Economy and Theology

Economy and Theology: Cusanus's Theory of Value, a study from the field of the history of philosophy, responds to the present-day interest in what is referred to as economic theology. This study aims to show that value (*valor*), one of the fundamental concepts of contemporary philosophy and economics, has its genealogy in the thought of Nicholas of Cusa. Starting from the economic context (the concept of price/*pretium*), Cusanus proposes the theory of value that, on the one hand, is objectively rooted in the Divine act of creation (God as the Minter) and, on the other hand, requires reading by human beings (human mind as a banker). While this theory appears in Cusanus's late work *The Bowling-Game*, it is underpinned by his theory of knowledge, theory of human beings and human cognition against the background of his vision of the universe. Thus, the aim of the book is to try to answer the question about the role and tasks of human beings as a principal player in economic and social game. This description of human position emerges from the creative tension between human philosophical and theological reflection and certain economic solutions.

Agnieszka Kijewska is tenure professor at the Chair of History of Ancient and Medieval Philosophy in Philosophical Faculty, John Paul II Lublin Catholic University, Poland.

Economics and Humanities
Series Editor: Sebastian Berger
University of the West of England (UWE Bristol), UK

The *Economics and Humanities* series presents the economic wisdom of the humanities and arts. Its volumes gather the economic senses sheltered and revealed by some of the most excellent sources within philosophy, poetry, art and story-telling. By re-rooting economics in its original domain these contributions allow economic phenomena and their meanings to come into the open more fully; indeed, they allow us to ask anew the question "What is economics?" Economic truth is thus shown to arise from the Human rather than the Market.

Readers will gain a foundational understanding of a humanities-based economics and find their economic sensibility enriched. They should turn to this series if they are interested in questions such as: What are the economic consequences of rooting economic Truth in the Human? What is the purpose of a humanities-based economics? What is the proper meaning of the "oikos", and how does it arise? What are the true meanings of wealth and poverty, gain and loss, capital and productivity? In what sense is economic reasoning with words more fundamental than reasoning with numbers? What is the dimension and measure of human dwelling in the material world?

These volumes address themselves to all those who are interested in sources and foundations for economic wisdom. Students and academics who are fundamentally dissatisfied with the state of economics and worried that its crisis undermines society will find this series of interest.

Capitalism and Christianity
Origins, Spirit and Betrayal of the Market Economy
Luigino Bruni

Economy and Theology
Cusanus's Theory of Value
Agnieszka Kijewska

For more information about this series, please visit: www.routledge.com/ Economics-and-Humanities/book-series/RSECH

Economy and Theology
Cusanus's Theory of Value

Agnieszka Kijewska
Translated by Roman Majeran

Routledge
Taylor & Francis Group

LONDON AND NEW YORK

First published 2024
by Routledge
4 Park Square, Milton Park, Abingdon, Oxon OX14 4RN

and by Routledge
605 Third Avenue, New York, NY 10158

Routledge is an imprint of the Taylor & Francis Group, an informa business

British Library Cataloguing-in-Publication Data
A catalogue record for this book is available from the British Library

ISBN: 978-1-032-31515-7 (hbk)
ISBN: 978-1-032-31648-2 (pbk)
ISBN: 978-1-003-31069-3 (ebk)

DOI: 10.4324/9781003310693

Typeset in Sabon LT Pro
by KnowledgeWorks Global Ltd.

To my friend, Roman Majeran, PhD, exceptional translator, thanks to whose assistance my texts, including this book, have appeared and are available in English.

Contents

Abbreviations

Ap   NICHOLAS OF CUSA. *A defence of Learned Ignorance*,
in: *Nicholas of Cusa's Debate with John Wenck*, trans.
by J. Hopkins, The Arthur J. Banning Press, Minneapolis,
1981. pp. 459–492 (Apologia12-2000.pdf [jasper-hopkins.
info]).

AT   *Concerning the Loftiest Level of Contemplative Reflection*,
trans. by J. Hopkins, in: *Nicholas of Cusa: Metaphysical
Speculations,* The Arthur J. Banning Press, Minneapolis,
1998. pp. 1423–1442 (DeApice12-2000.pdf (jasper-hopkins.
info).

C   *Compendium*, trans. by Jasper Hopkins, in: *Nicholas of Cusa
on Wisdom and Knowledge,* The Arthur J. Banning Press,
Minneapolis, 1996. pp. 1386–1419 (Compendium12-2000.pdf
[jasper-hopkins.info]).

CC   *The Catholic Concordance*, ed. by P. E. Sigmund, Cambridge
University Press, Cambridge, 1991.

DB   *On [intellectual] eyeglasses*, trans. by J. Hopkins, in: *Nicholas
of Cusa: Metaphysical Speculations,* The Arthur J. Banning
Press, Minneapolis, 1998. pp. 792–838 (DeBeryllo12-2000.pdf
[jasper-hopkins.info]).

DC   *On Surmises*, in: *Nicholas of Cusa: Metaphysical Speculations:
Volume Two*, trans. by J. Hopkins, The Arthur J. Banning
Press, Minneapolis, 2000. pp. 163–297 (DeConi12-2000
[jasper-hopkins.info]).

DF   *On being a Son of God*, in: *A Miscellany on Nicholas of
Cusa,* trans. by J. Hopkins, The Arthur J. Banning Press,
Minneapolis, 1994. pp. 341–369 (DeFiliatione12-2000.pdf
[jasper-hopkins.info]).

DI   *On Learned Ignorance*, trans. by J. Hopkins, 2nd ed., The
Arthur J. Banning Press, Minneapolis, 1985 (DI-I-12-2000.pdf
[jasper-hopkins.info]).

DM   *The Layman on Mind*, trans. by J. Hopkins, in: *Nicholas of Cusa on Wisdom and Knowledge,* The Arthur J. Banning Press, Minneapolis, 1996. pp. 531–601 (DeMente12-2000.pdf [jasper-hopkins.info]).

DP   *On Actualized-possibility*, trans. by J. Hopkins, University of Minnesota Press, Minneapolis, 1978.

DS   *The Layman on Wisdom*, trans. by J. Hopkins, in: *Nicholas of Cusa on Wisdom and Knowledge*, The Arthur J. Banning Press, Minneapolis, 1996. pp. 497–526 (DeSap12-2000.pdf [jasper-hopkins.info]).

LG   *The Bowling-Game*, trans. by J. Hopkins, in: *Nicholas of Cusa: Metaphysical Speculations: Volume Two,* The Arthur J. Banning Press, Minneapolis, 2000. pp. 1182–1274 (DeLudo12-2000.pdf [jasper-hopkins.info]).

NA   *On Non-other*, trans. by J. Hopkins, in: *Nicholas of Cusa on God as Not-other. A Translation and an Appraisal of De Li Non Aliud,* 3rd ed., The Arthur J. Banning Press, Minneapolis, 1987. pp. 1108–1178 (NA12-2000.pdf [jasper-hopkins.info]).

PF   *On Peaceful Unity of Faith*, trans. by J. Hopkins, 2nd ed., The Arthur J. Banning Press, Minneapolis, 1994. pp. 633–676 (DePace12-2000.pdf [jasper-hopkins.info]).

S-1   *Nicholas of Cusa's Early Sermons: 1430-1441,* trans. by J. Hopkins, The Arthur J. Banning Press, Loveland, Colorado, 2003 (CusaEarlySerintro.pdf [jasper-hopkins.info]).

S-2   *Nicholas of Cusa's Didactic Sermons: A Selection,* trans. by J. Hopkins, The Arthur J. Bannings Press, Loveland, Colorado, 2008 (FinalSelectSermons front matter.qxp [jasper-hopkins.info]).

S-3   *Nicholas of Cusa's Last Sermons (1457-1463),* trans. by J. Hopkins, 2011 (Preface & Introduction [jasper-hopkins.info]).

VD   *The Vision of God*, trans. by J. Hopkins, in: *Nicholas of Cusa's Dialectical Mysticism,* 3rd ed., The Arthur J. Banning Press, Minneapolis, 1985. pp. 679–743 (dialectical mysticism q 12-2000.qxd [jasper-hopkins.info]).

VS   *On the Pursuit of Wisdom*, trans. by J. Hopkins, in: *Nicholas of Cusa: Metaphysical Speculations*, The Arthur J. Banning Press, Minneapolis, 1998. pp. 1278–1381 (VS12-2000.pdf [jasper-hopkins.info]).

1 Introductory circles of history of philosophy and economic theology

History of medieval philosophy

As a historian of ancient and medieval philosophy, in my research I mostly concerned myself with the history of Neoplatonism in mature Christian antiquity and the Latin Middle Ages, that is to say with the thought of St. Augustine, Boethius, John Scotus Eriugena, the so-called School of Chartres and, finally, Nicholas of Cusa. On the other hand, during my philosophical studies, I was formed in the spirit of the approach to the medieval philosophical thought which has been described by John Inglis as the Neoscholastic paradigm of medieval studies, the method originated by Joseph Kleutgen and Albert Stöckl, who "invented" such discipline as history of medieval philosophy.[1] This approach and method appealed to many students of medieval intellectual life and additional boost to developing medieval studies came from Pope Leo XIII, who in his encyclical *Aeterni Patris* of 1879 encouraged scholars to take up the study of the Fathers of the Church and the intellectual traditions of the Middle Ages. The efforts to rediscover and assimilate the imposing legacy of the past Christian thought continued, with chief contributions coming from Martin Grabmann, Etienné Gilson and Maurice de Wulf; in Poland, this approach to the legacy of medieval intellectual life was introduced by Stefan Swieżawski, a student of Gilson and Jacques Maritain. I will not discuss here in detail the essence of the Neoscholastic paradigm of historical studies since I have done it elsewhere.[2] Nevertheless, to highlight its most essential features, I will mention the four basic questions which invariably guided the practitioners of that paradigm in their research. These questions are as follows:

(A) "In what way was the conjunction of faith and reason effected in medieval philosophy?"[3]; (B) "How did medieval authors seek to develop the epistemology based on the conception of human natural cognitive faculties"[4]; (C) What was "the contribution of medieval authors to the development of some standard domains of philosophical

DOI: 10.4324/9781003310693-1

inquiry, especially those, where the inspirational role of the Christian doctrine is evident, such as natural theology, metaphysics, and anthropology?"[5]; (D) "What relation does a given philosopher or idea bear to the philosophy of Thomas Aquinas."[6]

The first attempts to break with the restrictive assumptions of this Neoscholastic approach came from within the circle of its practitioners: Philotheus Böhner voiced his dissatisfaction at the failure of the scholarly opinion to give its due to the philosophy of William Ockham, and Fernand Van Steenberghen found it suitable to depart from the mapping of the philosophical currents in the Latin 13th century worked out by Franz Ehrle and Pierre Mandonnet.[7] From another point of view, it was observed that medieval science, in particular medicine, played an important role in shaping the development of philosophical ideas by paving the way for new philosophical influences and bringing about doctrinal innovations. This was the point made by my philosophy teacher, Marian Kurdziałek, who continued the work in that field of his master, Alexander Birkenmajer of the Jagiellonian University.[8]

An entirely new approach to the medieval philosophical legacy came from the tradition of analytical philosophy and found its first full-scale expression in the volume of *Cambridge History of Later Medieval Philosophy* edited by Norman Kretzmann, Anthony Kenny and Ian Pinborg in 1982.[9] In this volume, topics are selected and ordered by problems and not by chronology, and the choice of material is very significant: most chapters are devoted to logic instead of theology and metaphysics, logic having always been a privileged field of interest for analytical philosophers as the discipline providing the formal tools and structures necessary for any scientific and philosophical research. This structuring of historical philosophical investigations according to problems rather than mere chronology seems to be a novel and valuable contribution of this volume and the whole approach it originates.

Among the alternative approaches to the Neoscholastic paradigm to history of ancient and medieval philosophy that have emerged in the recent half-century, a very special position is occupied by Alain de Libera, who describes his approach to medieval studies as "relativist, holistic, and proclaiming discontinuity," also as "methodical Foucaultism" avoiding both exaggeration and skepticism.[10] In his research, de Libera makes use of the idea of *translatio studiorum*, borrowed from Paul Vignaux and from other areas of historical studies. In his opinion, the medieval world had no definite center either politically or intellectually: what informed the developments in the Arab world in the 11th century would only become significant for Europe in the 12/13th century. What we can observe and register is the shifting (*translatio*) of texts, ideas, currents and styles of philosophical thinking between diverse political and intellectual centers.[11] However, the problems and philosophical verities that are thus "translated" between various milieux are never eternal philosophical concerns or truths (*philosophia perennis*), and the role of historico-philosophical study is to follow the "genealogy" of a given problem, and it may very often be the case that in the concrete development of a philosophical position a false answer could be of more significance than a discovered truth.[12]

A very pertinent observation on the nature of the philosophical study of past ideas came from Philipp Rosemann. He rightly claims that there is no history of philosophy without some underlying philosophical assumptions, which implicitly determine the interpretation of the studied facts; thus, every generation of scholars has to write its own version of the past development of philosophical ideas.[13] Our contemporary way of thinking is highly distrustful of any totalizing syntheses, regardless of their inspiration, whether Thomist, Marxist or Hegelian. It is no longer considered viable to reduce all manifold expressions of thought to one style of thinking, regarded as basic or privileged for some reason; we readily accept the idea that there is more than just one model of rationality. In general, the contemporary philosophy and culture lays heavy emphasis on variety and diversity. However, given this attitude, how can we avoid the trap of relativism? It is precisely medieval philosophy, Rosemann claims, that has a relevant answer to this question. It teaches us that in our cognitive endeavors we should strive after absolute and complete truth, yet we should be aware that we cannot perfectly achieve that truth here and now and by our finite and imperfect means. The method the medievals pursued the truth in philosophy and theology suggests an approach that both recognizes the absolute value of truth while trying to give justice to all legitimate partial and one-sided points of view. This method was the scholastic *quaestio*.[14] By bringing into confrontation diverse, often opposed, points of view, by introducing necessary distinctions and divisions, one strove to grasp the truth uniting all incomplete insights and being the common achievement of all the participants in the debate.

This description of the medieval approach to the human quest for truth applies in a particular way to Nicholas of Cusa, a thinker of the borderline between the Middle Ages and the Renaissance.[15] True, he no longer pursued the method of the scholastic question, but his approach to the problems he discussed in his works remained dialectical and, so to say, dialogical through and through. He, too, compared and confronted with one another diverse opinions on the matter in question and did not shy away from apparent paradoxes, and by this means, he strove to achieve a higher level insight into the truth of the subject. In a way that looks very modern, he thought the absolute and precise truth to remain forever unachievable to our finite cognitive efforts, which, however, by no means implies that the knowledge we can naturally gain is without value. He described human knowledge as conjecture (*coniectura*); that is, as cognition that is true in its legitimate scope yet limited to a particular point of view and, as such, always open to further completion by incorporating other viewpoints. In this way, Cusanus's thought is, by virtue of its very basic assumption, made immune to the danger of totalization. This is one of the salient aspects of his philosophy I would like to emphasize in my presentation of his thought, alongside its dialectical and dialogical character, its openness to further completion and its essential involvement with paradox. My philosophical education in a Neoscholastic milieu left me with the belief in the importance of partitioning the thought of a given philosopher under discussion into separate domains, such as theory of being, anthropology and epistemology, and I intend to hold to this assumption in this book. Nevertheless, I drop some distinctions dear to the Neoscholastic paradigm, and above all, I will no longer observe the strict separation of the orders of faith and reason and philosophy and theology, the reason for this being that such distinctions are totally absent from Cusanus's own discussions, which tend to follow the Boethian methodology based on the assumption that theology is the "innermost part of philosophy."

Among the fundamental domains of philosophical reflection, philosophical anthropology is, I believe, of particular importance for the comprehension and explication of Cusanus's thought, and this is not only because of the historical context of his activity, marked by the ascendancy of humanism, but also, above all, because of the inner concern of his philosophy. Hans Blumenberg spoke of the principal interests of his philosophy as forming a triangle, whose vertices are man, God and the cosmos.[16]

Medieval science, whatever we may think of it, was also instrumental in shaping the development of medieval philosophy. The reception of Aristotelianism in the 12/13th century had been preceded and prepared by the medical milieux taking interest in Aristotelian natural science, as shown by Birkenmajer.[17] Cusanus himself possessed a rich collection of medical manuscripts.[18] He was interested in practicing medicine and is even credited with the invention of a new method of feeling the pulse; however, the disciplines that had a profound influence on and occupied special place in his mind were mathematical sciences. Mathematics had been advocated as a necessary and very efficient preparation for the study of divine things by the Pythagorean-Platonic tradition. There is no unanimous agreement among Cusanus scholars on how innovative he was in his cosmology; while some maintain that his conception was truly original, others think that he mostly built upon the work of his predecessors. There is no doubt, however, that his approach to every kind of scientific study was based on mathematics and the disciplines of quadrivium and as such it was very original and foreshadowed the modern scientific methodology. His investigations into the structure of the Universe served more than one purpose, the fact I will return to in the appropriate place in this book.

Mathematical concepts are decidedly privileged in Cusanus's writings but are far from being the only kind of objects he uses as symbols to convey the meaning of the profound and abstruse insights into the transcendent reality gained in the course of his investigations. Given his predominant concern with the reality of the transcendent, it is no wonder that he makes extensive use of symbolism and metaphors in his writings; he himself characterized the method of his own philosophy as "symbolic investigation."[19] Recently Peter T. Struck has drawn attention to the importance of the broadly conceived symbol in the study of ancient literature (*symbolon,* allegory, *hyponoia* – conjecture and *ainigma* – riddle). The use of imagery in speech or writing encourages one to go beyond the narrow literal sense of the message and interpret it allegorically, with new, often surprising, possibilities of meaning being unexpectedly unveiled.[20] It is in this perspective that Hans Blumenberg read Cusanus's texts and interpreted his thought.[21]

In Nicholas's philosophical pedagogy, symbols and metaphors play a crucial role as parenetic and anagogical devices. He typically starts with some concrete reality, as for instance a game, a spoon or a prism and by considering its qualities conducts the reader along the ascending path of increasingly abstract and spiritual discussion up to the level of "sublime speculation." In this book, I will discuss more closely not only some of Cusanus's metaphors, such as that of the game, the ball, but also the symbol of man as microcosm and such economic metaphors as that of the relationship between the coin-maker, banker and the coin.

Having accepted de Libera's suggestion that medieval philosophy lacks a definite center and its development consists in the shifting of philosophical problems between diverse political and cultural milieux, with the questions, words and statements losing old and acquiring new meanings in new contexts, I accepted the idea that the domain of economic theology could be an interesting area of speculation providing a novel and interesting perspective upon Cusanus's intellectual vision as a whole. Thus, I decided to accept the editors' proposal and explore the problem, what new light the analysis of economic theology as found in Cusanus's writings can throw on the whole of his thought.[22]

Economic theology

As Paul Oslington observed, many problems discussed in the domains of economics, sociology, philosophy, theology and history resulted in the emergence of a new, interdisciplinary area of research, combining economy and theology.[23] The editor of *The Routledge Handbook of*

Economic Theology of 2020 applied the name of *economic theology* to that new discipline. Stefan Schwarzkopf opens the volume with *an introduction to economic theology* in which he states as follows:

> Economics and business administration, too, have recently been exposed to a theological turn of their own. Among the many ways to conceptualize this exposure, the term "economic theology" suggests itself as a way to reconfigure theorizing the economy around the role that theology played in shaping economic concepts and the social presence of the sacred in economic life. Economic theology, although a relatively new term, can be considered a research field with intellectual roots stretching all the way back to Karl Marx, Max Weber, (…) and Walter Benjamin. It comprises a *methodological* and *theoretical* component. The first component provides the tools to investigate the relationship between theology and economic concepts and practices. The second component claims that particular economic practices, behaviours, concepts and institutions are in fact not just grounded in theological concerns over justice and personal transformation, but that this grounding actually renders economic practices, institutions and economic thought *as such* a part of the realm of the sacred.[24]

Further on in the introduction, the author attempts to define this new field of study by specifying its domain, which is conceived broadly enough to encompass the past as well as the present. Schwarzkopf's proposed definition of economic theology goes as follows:

> It is the study of the forms of interaction between theological imaginaries on the one hand, and economic thought and economic-managerial practices on the other, both past and present. It identifies explicit and implicit theologies inherent in economic concepts, institutions and practices as well as the role of economic terminology within theological thought, both past and present.[25]

All kinds of interaction between theological imagination on one side and economic theory and practice on the other are regarded as qualifying for discussion within this new area of research: explicit borrowings and references as well as implicit and hidden influences; all kinds of relationships between conceptual structures in the domains under consideration are of interest: whether they be relations of analogy, homology or resonance of a kind.[26] An excellent example of research done within thus conceived economic theology, and the noteworthy results produced by it is Devin Singh's book *Divine Currency. The Theological*

Power of Money in the West (2018). The author of the book describes his work as an occupation in theological genealogy, archaeology of economics and a re/constructive theology. He states as follows:

> This study contributes to a theological genealogy of economy in the West. A full-fledged genealogy would require a multivolume work that traces the emergence and permutations of the ideas I survey as they shape late antique, medieval, and modern society. I engage here in archaeological retrieval of key founding tropes in the early Christian imaginary. I do so fully cognizant that archaeological work, as situated *description* of a perceived past, is simultaneously a type of construction and is, hence, *redescription*.[27]

The author provides further elucidation by enlarging on the meaning of genealogy and archaeology, their functioning in philosophical and historical research and how they are different from traditional ways of studying social phenomena. In doing this, he clearly draws, just as Alain de Libera did in his reflections on history of philosophy, on the thought and vocabulary of Michel Foucault:

> Genealogy challenges assumptions about the historian as a fixed, sovereign subject and objective observer of the past. It questions historical approaches that serve "as the handmaiden to philosophy," vindicating timeless truths rather than analysing the past in all its complexity. Genealogy subverts the quest for origins, interrogating the drive for an original, pure moment of a phenomenon, something untainted by materiality and change. Instead, it strives to highlight the diverse and often conflicting ensemble of elements associated with a certain manifestation of a phenomenon. (...). Rigorous archaeology means examining not merely a certain idea but also the material practices, institution, symbolic media, and political and economic formations that experience, shape, and manifest it.[28]

According to Stefan Schwarzkopf, this new field of study which is economic theology has a significant role to play in our contemporary efforts better to understand cultural and social phenomena; he observes as follows:

> First, most histories of economic thought often briefly mention Xenophon and Aristotle, and then cold-start their narratives with Adam Smith, as if the 2,000-odd years of intellectual history in between did not matter. Second, the role that economy has obtained today as the realm in which a quasi-providential plan of improvement and

growth unfolds itself – if left alone by obnoxious bureaucrats – can only be understood if one recognizes the *theological transformation* this concept experienced.[29]

In the book that follows, I would like to propose a contribution to the task of filling the gap Schwarzkopf mentions by presenting Nicholas of Cusa as a thinker who addressed in his own way matters of economics and combined this interest with his theological preoccupations and thus rightfully belongs in that long narrative which traces the genealogy of economic concepts. The work on the genealogy of economic notions in European tradition has been done mostly by Hannah Arendt, Michel Foucault and Giorgio Agamben; these authors explored mostly the legacy of the patristic and medieval thought. Nicholas of Cusa and his approach to economic matters promises to be a particularly interesting object of study, given his situation on the borderline between the Middle Ages and the Renaissance and modernity as a whole. In his thought, a number of themes initiated in medieval scholasticism are revived, yet his treatment of them is usually innovative and the context of his discussion foreshadows the approach of modern mentality. Possibly the exploration of this as yet largely unexplored object of analysis will contribute to the confirmation of Carl Schmitt's thesis that "all political-constitutional concepts are ultimately secularized theological concepts."[30] If so, the discovery of this mostly forgotten theological dimension of some of our economic and political concepts may encourage reconsidering these notions in a new light and endow them with new capacity to instruct and inspire.

One of those fundamental concepts is the very notion of *oikonomia,* whose roots go back to antiquity and which combines the meaning of the word *oikos* referring to a house/household and that of *nomos:* a law or regulation, thus the *oikonomia* signifying the art of ruling or managing a house. According to Dotan Leshem, the ancients thought of fundamental rational human activity as constituted in three domains, namely economics, politics and philosophy, although economics was not regarded as being on a par with the other two. As he states,

> Ancient philosophers held two of these activities as praiseworthy. These were philosophy and politics. At the same time, the indulgence in economic matters was despised, and was considered slavish and unmanly.[31]

Plato and, above all, Aristotle developed a conception of a political community modelled on that of the household: their *polis* being patterned after the *oikos* as being ideally, self-sufficient, versatile in terms of functions as well as social comprehensiveness, able to foster and governed by virtue. The close bond sought after in the practice of social life between economics, politics and philosophy is best illustrated by the example taken from Xenophon:

> According to this view, economic activity dealt with the satisfaction of the bare necessities of life and with the generation of surplus leisure time that was meant to allow the master of the household, the *oikodespotes,* to conduct a leisurely life, whether a philosophical or a political one. (...) Xenophon already brought together the philosophical (Socratic) and the political (sophist) arts of generating surplus in the *Oikonomikos.* (...) Socrates, the philosopher, does so by moderating his needs, while Ischomachus, the model citizen (*polites*), is praised as one of "those who are able not only to govern their own oikos but also to accumulate a surplus (...)."[32]

Dotan Leshem generalizes this example as illustrating the attitude held by most theorists in the ancient Greek-speaking world:

> Most philosophical schools in Greek-speaking antiquity (...) defined the economic sphere as one in which man, when faced with excessive means, acquires a theoretical and practical prudent disposition in order to comply with his needs and generate surplus that appears outside its boundaries.[33]

These thoughts would find ample resonance in Cusanus's own ideas, himself being a keen admirer of and seeker for manuscripts containing ancient texts. Together with his friend Cardinal Bessarion, he labored over the correction of the new translation of Plato's *Parmenides.*[34] His general intellectual attitude, open-minded and carefully critical at the same time, can be described as Socratic, and the efforts to imitate Socrates's example can be seen in his written output: the form of philosophical dialogue, which was one of Cusanus's favorite literary forms, was undoubtedly inspired by Plato's and Xenophon's attempts to represent their master's philosophical and didactic practice in the medium of writing. The situation in which Cusanus's dialogues are set may resemble that of Xenophon's and some Plato's: there is a figure of a mentor and that of a pupil, and the conversation takes on a decidedly parenetic or didactic character. Moreover, the pupils are typically young men of aristocratic background and probably of much political influence in the future, as in the dialogue of *The Bowling-Game,* where Cusanus's interlocutors are Prince John, son of Otto I Wittelsbach of Mosbach, and his relative, Prince of Bavaria, Albert IV. The starting point may be some concrete reality close at hand, as, in this dialogue, the bowling game much in vogue at the time: beginning with some features of the game, Cusanus the mentor develops the topic and attempts to lead his young partners to speculative heights where they can gain insights into the most elevated matters; he guides them all the way up to "sublime speculation" and exhorts them to practice virtues, as Xenophon's Socrates would have done. The term *oikonomia*, important for the Greco-Roman antiquity before Christ and its conception of the threefold human activity,[35] also appears in the Bible and the patristic tradition. The word itself and its derivatives are found in the Old Testament, yet it is only in the New Testament that it acquires a very special meaning of its own and lasting theological importance.[36] Even though it does not form the central theological concept of Pauline theology, according to Leshem, it was with St. Paul that it was first given the unmistakably theological interpretation:

> The origin of its meaning, as "dispensation of revealed divine mystery," is found in Paul's letter to the Ephesians.
> He made known to us the mystery of His will, according to His kind intention which He purposed in Him; with a view to an economy of the fullness of ages to recapitulate all in Christ, things in the heavens and thing on the earth.
>
> (Ephesians 1:9–10)

> To enlighten all what is the economy of the mystery which from eternity has been hid in God who created all things.
>
> (Ephesians 3:9)

> (...) Even if we were to accept the view that *oikonomia* does not mean the fulfilment of a neatly ordered divine plan in Paul's mind, at the very least it means the inner-worldly management of the divine mystery in accordance with God's intention.[37]

Thus in St. Paul and his epistle to Ephesians, we find the first fundamental meaning that the word *oikonomia* carries in the Bible; this is (1) the divine plan eternally existing in the Divine Mind and progressively revealed in God's works of creation and, particularly, of redemption by means of the special intervention of God in the history of mankind which was effected through the Incarnation. With the passage of time, the Incarnation of God in the man Jesus Christ came to be synonymous with the term "divine economy."

There are also other meanings attributed to the word *oikonomia* present in the ancient Christian context: one (2) is found in St. Justin Martyr and is explained as "immoral and otherwise unacceptable accommodation to the circumstances in order to achieve a sought-after goal."[38] Yet another (3) understanding of the word *oikonomia* was probably introduced by Tatian the Syrian and came to widespread use during the Arian controversy;

it referred to "the mode by which God the Father begets His Son, that is, the relationship between the Father and son in the Goodhead."[39]

In this book, I would like to take a close look at the way Cusanus takes up and transforms the three meanings of the word *oikonomia* as fixed in the patristic tradition and handed down to the medieval world. I intend to set his development of the many-sided notion of *oikonomia* in the context of and in its relationship to Cusanus's conception of the triple birth of the Divine Word, which he develops mainly in his sermons. The Word is born firstly within the Godhead as the Son of the Father, one of the Persons of the Holy Trinity; secondly, that same Word, the Person of the Trinity, is born as a human being in the act of Incarnation. The third birth of the Word takes place in the hearts of those who, through their faith, became sons of God. It is immediately noticeable that the birth of the Word of the Father corresponds to the third meaning of *oikonomia* (the one introduced by Tertullian), while the birth of the Incarnate Word is the fulfilment of the divine plan of salvation for humankind eternally existing in God's mind, which is precisely the meaning of "divine economy" as used by St. Paul. The birth of the Word in the souls of the faithful Christians is the same as taking on the likeness to Christ (*Christiformitas*), being made a son of God (*filiatio*) and seeing God (*theosis*). The birth of the Word a human soul should prevent the human being from realizing in his/her life the second meaning of *oikonomia* found in the patristic literature, that is from accommodating to the world of sin rather than transforming this world according to God's will.

The method of economic theology, the characteristic tool of it, is historical and linguistic research aiming at retracing the development and reconstructing genealogies of the concepts, tactics and strategies, which, having originated in the sphere of economics, came to be meaningfully used within the broadly conceived spheres of religion and theology. One of the results of this kind of study is gaining a theoretical insight into the truth that Schwarzkopf drew attention to, namely that viewing various aspects of economic life in a theological perspective accompanied by careful attention to justice, self-development and reformation of one's attitude "renders economic practices, institutions and economic thought *as such* a part of the realm of the sacred."[40]

That ordinary human occupations and activities can be intimately related to the realm of the sacred is an idea very close to Nicholas of Cusa's thought; one good illustration of this is his having taken an ordinary game of ball as a starting point for and an illustration of a lofty philosophical consideration, a speculative effort to penetrate into the sublime sphere of the sacred. In this way a simple human pastime becomes a kind of liturgy, a ceremony, which in a way realizes that which it illustrates.

A game, like a liturgical ritual, requires a specially assigned space and a time set aside for the purpose; that time has to be free of all other occupations, and it has to be an *otium*. Moreover, a game must have set principles and rules, and successful participation in it requires training and effort. The purpose of participating in a game is to win, and to become the winner is to achieve a sort of fulfilment, to actualize some part of one's potential and to realize some value.

Schwarzkopf observes as follows:

> The command 'work harder' is *theologically* significant since it does not simply call on followers to get rich quick. Rather, working harder means to live more intensively the realization that one is 'in the world but not of the world'.[41]

In the light of the above statement, and guided by Cusanus's mystagogic explorations of games and other daily life phenomena, we will be invited to ask ourselves searching questions concerning the essence of human fulfilment and perfect self-realization. Today, how do we represent to ourselves the perfect fulfilment of human essential strivings, the ultimate end of all human endeavors? Have the recent trying and calamitous global events of pandemic and economic crisis changed our vision of the world and our place therein? Much of our confidence has been shaken during the last decade: despite the apparent rapid progress in medical sciences, the Covid outbreak claimed millions of victims worldwide and we are still ignorant both of the far-reaching effects of the disease and of the effective cure for it. The war in the Ukraine rudely put an end to our naive belief that Europe has outgrown the age of great armed conflicts and now all Europeans are unanimous in their acceptance of the superior values of peace and human dignity. Nor could the belief in the power of economic measures to assuage or even stop political conflicts stand the test of the events of the last decade: international laws and institutions turned out to be unable to prevent mass acts of violence – robberies, murders and tortures. War in one part of the world intensified poverty and famine in other parts, thus raising once again questions about justice conceived as equitable distribution of necessary goods for human existence and well-being. But again, is the adequate provision of consumer goods enough to secure fulfilment and perfect well-being to human beings? In her excellent book *Wandering in Darkness*, Eleonore Stump makes the following observation:

> Being in a flourishing condition is also what a person cares about, even if he does not know what exactly flourishing is for him, even if he does not know that he does not know, even if he thinks he knows but is mistaken. (...) Accordingly, there are two different elements in what a person cares about, a subjective element and an objective element. On the one hand, what a person cares about is equivalent to that person's

well-being, objectively understood, to her flourishing and being the best she can be. Understood in this way, what a person cares about is what she ought to be. (...) On the other hand, what a person cares about is what has great value for her in virtue of her commitment to it.[42]

Nicholas of Cusa does address the ever-present questions of the highest value, the ultimate end of all human endeavors and the true source of the well-being of humanity, and one of the pedagogical means he uses is to put under scrutiny the structure and movements of a human pastime, the bowling game, taken by him to be an example and illustration of human endeavor in general. In what follows, I will subject his work *The Bowling-Game* to detailed discussion. In this work, Cusanus introduces the concept of value (*valor*), whose origin lies in the sphere of economics and which derives from the notion of the price (*pretium*). Some value or goodness inheres in any thing in the world, and all of these particular values are ultimately grounded in the Absolute Value. To make this point clear and convincing, Cusanus again employs an illustration taken from ordinary life; this time, it is a standard economic practice of using coined money. God, the all-powerful Coin-Maker produces a coin by impressing a similitude of His own Substance, his Son on a piece of matter. The value of this coin and the extension of its circulation do not depend on the matter used for its production; it wholly derives from the impressed likeness of the Ruler. This ingenious simile shows how the divine *oikonomia* works: God puts his design into execution through "monetary incarnation."[43] Man, the Banker, is the indispensable partner in this structured economic situation: although it is the Coin-Maker who informs the coin and decides its true value, it is the Banker who recognizes the likeness in the coin, evaluates it and puts it into circulation. Moreover, man, who participates in this implementation of the divine economy, increasingly takes on the likeness of the archetypal coin – the Christ – and becomes himself a coin with intrinsic value of its own. In a way, to use another economic term, one could say that the purpose of this divine *oikonomia* is multiplication and perfection of existing valuable resources, both in an individual and universal perspective.

The allegory of the Coin-Maker, coined money and the Banker is an example of Cusanus's pedagogical device of introducing the reader to the consideration of increasingly abstruse and elevated, fundamental problems of the structure of the world, man's place within the Universe, the structure of man himself and the mode and preconditions of human cognition. Cusanus's preferred pedagogy is that of "leading by the hand" (*manuductio*) from the commonplace and ordinary, yet familiar and obvious, to the removed and sublime, and ultimately definitive of the human condition.

A comprehension of the structure of the Universe is a necessary component part of this pedagogy: for one thing, the Universe is the proper dwelling place (*oikos*) of man, and for another, the very structure of man and the social institutions formed by man and for man are, or should be, modelled on the universal cosmic pattern. The last statement sums up the meaning of the traditional conception of man as microcosm. As Marian Kurdziałek has shown, the ancient conception of man as an image and a diminished copy of the Universe, originating with Democritus and Plato, found varied reception in the thought of the Middle Ages.[44] Generally, it was assumed that not only the structure of the human body, of the human soul and of the human being as a whole was patterned after the universal cosmic order but also the structure of various social bodies and human institutions, in particular of the state. Cusanus took up the theme of human reality as a microcosm and following the Stoic philosopher Hierocles represented human activity within this world as a game consisting in attempting to get to the center of a system of concentric circles:

> Around one's mind, regarded as the center, there runs a series of ever wider concentric circles, beginning with that representing one's own body; then moving outward to circles representing one's parents, siblings, spouse, and children; on to more remote relatives; and then to members of the same *deme* and tribe, to fellow citizens, to those who belong to the same people or *ethnos*, until one arrives at the widest circle, which is that of the entire human race. The width of the circles and their distance from the center constitute the standard by which to measure the intensity of one's ties, and therefore of one's "duties" or "appropriate acts" toward people."[45]

Human life being viewed as a sort of game, it is structured and organized like one. There is a goal to achieve, some kind of fulfilment. Like a game, human life is organized along certain principles that have to be learned and assimilated by the player, and this requires acquisition of some knowledge and appropriate training. The center to be reached is "in the world," but not "of the world," for only a transcendent end can satisfy human thirst for fulfilment.

Spiritual exercise

In this place, I would like to refer to a certain conception of philosophy and philosophizing which I find particularly helpful in the discussion and presentation of the thought of Nicholas of Cusa; this is the conception of philosophy as spiritual exercise formulated by Pierre Hadot and later modified by Michel Foucault. According to Hadot's idea, any sincere effort at philosophical understanding of reality and the human place within it is not merely a detached theoretical speculation that leaves untouched the deeper layers of personality, but an act that reaches into the core of one's spiritual identity and transforms the way one thinks, feels and acts, indeed the way one realizes one's existence as a human being. To anyone familiar with Cusanus's philosophical works, it is clear that his whole speculative effort perfectly corresponds to Hadot's description of philosophy; it is an untiring search for fulfilment, a dialectical progress, in which passing through different limited points of view, adopting and transcending different one-sided perspectives, we constantly approach the absolute center, where we can hope to find the perfect fulfilment. The circles of the game, like Hierocles's spheres, represent the different realms of theoretical insight which must be explored and synthesized by the philosopher-player in his/her ascent to the vision of the supreme, Absolute Value.

Viewing the ancient philosophy of Greeks and Romans, mainly pagan, but also Christian, as Hadot did, in terms of spiritual exercise, has proved very fruitful and brought rich insights into the spirituality of the ancients. The approach to philosophy as an act involving and transforming the whole personality of a philosopher reveals the essential connection between the theoretical and practical components of philosophizing. The theoretical element is the indispensable foundation of a philosophical act; it provides the comprehension of the basic structure of the world (physics) and man's place therein; yet the purpose and consummation of philosophy as viewed by the ancients is practical and its aspirations are maximalist: it is no less than metamorphosis of the whole human personality. This is effected by constant efforts to transcend one's particular situation and the limitations involved in it, by overcoming one's subjective point of view and rising instead to God's/Providential/Nature's perspective on things, including the essential reference to the sphere of values.[46]

Many students of antiquity adopted the view that ancient philosophy can and ought to be studied and interpreted in terms of therapy of the evils of life (Martha Nussbaum).[47] For Hadot, the therapy of inauthentic attitudes, false convictions and that which provides the ground for both – passions – is but one aspect of the overall transforming function of philosophy. Hadot divides the process of the transformations accomplished by means of philosophical spiritual exercises into the following stages: (1) learning to live, (2) learning to converse with others, (3) learning to die and (4) learning to read.[48] Among the many ancient personages who came to be regarded as paragons of philosophical life, Socrates undoubtedly occupies the place of honor and can be considered the true master of philosophy as spiritual exercise.

In the above I already made the observation that Socratism appears to be an essential characteristic of Cusanus's philosophical attitude. Like Socrates, the Cardinal of St. Peter in Chains finds in a parenetic dialogue an efficient means of engaging his interlocutors and his readers in a search after wisdom. An indispensable introductory stage of this search and a condition for further fruitful participation in the dialogue is clear realization of one's own lack of wisdom, an act which opens to the participant the way to the stage of "learned unknowing." Socrates appears here as a perfect example of that crucial step on the way to wisdom. Hadot, referring to Socrates's celebrated confession of his own ignorance ("I know that I know nothing") emphasizes one particular aspect of the Athenian wise man's unknowing:

> This statement could be interpreted as meaning that Socrates did not possess any transmissible knowledge, and was unable to cause ideas to pass from his mind into that of others. (...) To be sure, Socrates was a passionate lover of words and dialogue. With just as much passion, however, he sought to demonstrate to us the limits of language. What he wanted to show us is that we can never understand justice if we do not live it.[49]

An essential characteristic of parenetic search for truth in a dialogue is that the truth one seeks to discover is not a merely theoretical constatation but an insight that has profound existential significance for the persons concerned. This insight is essentially related to the sphere of values that guide and direct human life; it is by far not enough to acquire some speculative knowledge of these values: true comprehension of values consists in living by them, by adopting them as the guiding light and principle of one's life and by being a "witness" (in Greek *martyr*) to them before others.

Although Socrates declares his own ignorance, he at the same time claims to have a very special relationship to those who are capable of coming to knowledge themselves: he can help them to "give birth" to knowledge in themselves, just like a midwife helps women to bear their children; thus, he claims to be a kind of midwife himself as it is shown in Plato's *Theaetetus*.[50]

Nicholas of Cusa, while inspiring his interlocutors to enter the path of intellectual speculation, encourages them first of all to discover the presuppositions of their own knowledge. The first a *priori* presupposition underlying and grounding every act of knowing, the "concept of concepts," is the notion of God. Yet acquiring awareness of all the a priori presuppositions conditioning human cognition and the inapparent way they function to produce the mechanism of human knowing is only made possible by taking a penetrating introspective look into the depths of one's own spiritual being; in other words, it requires a serious attempt and effort to come to the knowledge of oneself. Thus, "know thyself," the supreme maxim of ancient wisdom, appears in Cusanus's thought as the fundamental principle of his own search for wisdom.

The knowledge of oneself gained in the process of the search for wisdom should bring salutary fruits for an individual: it should set one working to achieve inner transformation, bringing an order into one's desires, unification (*at-onement*) of the inner self, acquisition of virtues, eradication or straightening of improper inclinations. This process of the inner transformation of the self has often been described as the process of learning to die.

Rowan Williams, who by analogy to Hadot's conception of philosophy as a spiritual exercise treated of theology as a form of spiritual exercise, observed,

> Theology as a way of life, therefore, involves at least three significant elements. It must be accompanied by a real growth in 'literacy' about oneself – a willingness to recognize the patterns of desire and imagination which, for good or ill, shape what is said. It must be marked by a profound patience with what *resists* being said, a patience both with my own inarticulacy and with the stumbling articulation of those with whom I am speaking. And it must, therefore, be committed to a conversational engagement with others seeking the same level of meaning, an openness to the discernment of others inside and outside community (because not everyone who seeks this level of meaning, the level at which God's purposes and human speech and action coincide, will automatically share the same believing vocabulary).[51]

In the quoted passage, besides the theme of acquiring self-knowledge, another important element of spiritual exercises is emphasized: exchange of insights in a dialogue with others similarly engaged in the quest for meaning, searching for truth in a community with fellow seekers. The truth we are all after is always greater than our particular insights into it, so, while we approach it, we can never claim to have grasped the ultimate "precise truth." The awareness of this fact should invite us to exercise patience toward ourselves and toward others. In his description of "theology as a way of life," Rowan Williams gets so close to the spirit of Cusanus as to say something that might have been said by the Cardinal himself:

> 'Theology as a way of life' is, ultimately and simply, an aspect of the life of 'filiation.'[52]

As I undertake in this book a journey across the circles of the Bishops of Brixen game of life, I will, understandably, begin with those which, according to Hierocles, are the closest to every human being, namely the circles of the family, friends and educators and the places where he studied and matured. Then, I will move to his literary production and his activity as a dignitary of the Church. I will follow up this general presentation with a more detailed discussion of the work *The Bowling-Game*, its outline and some aspects related to selected characteristic features of the game. The concluding chapters will discuss some questions of cosmology, philosophical theology and anthropology, that is the circles furthest removed from the human ego, yet whose integration within the sphere of one's personality means a successful accomplishment of the game of life and the perfect fulfilment of human development.

Notes

1 Cf. JOHN INGLIS, *Spheres of Philosophical Inquiry and the Historiography of Medieval Philosophy*, Brill, Leiden-Köln-Boston, 1998, pp. 10–11.
2 Cf. AGNIESZKA KIJEWSKA. "The history of medieval philosophy and its historiography." in: *Paradigms-Thinking Styles-Research Programs. How does science change?* eds. L. Kostuch, B. Wojciechowska, S. Konarska-Zimnicka, P. Tambor, University of Jan Kochanowski Press, Kielce, 2020, pp. 27–42.
3 There, p. 29.
4 There, p. 31.
5 There.
6 There, p. 32.
7 Cf. There, pp. 36–37.
8 On Fr Prof. Marian Kurdziałek's editorial and interpretive work done on medieval scientific texts, see AGNIESZKA KIJEWSKA. "Anthropology of Gilbertus Anglicus' 'Compendium medicinae'." in: *The Embodied Soul. Aristotelian Psychology and Physiology in Medieval Europe between 1200 and 1420*, eds. M. Gensler, M. Mansfeld, M. Michałowska, Springer, Cham, Switzerland, 2022, pp. 37–56.
9 This approach is continued in ROBERT PASNAU, CHRISTINA VAN DYCKE (eds.). *The Cambridge History of Medieval Philosophy*, Cambridge University Press, Cambridge, 2010.
10 Cf. ALAIN DE LIBERA. "Le relativisme historique: théorie des *complexes questions résponses* et *tratabilité*." *Les Etudés philosophiques*, 4, 1999, p. 484.
11 Cf. ALAIN DE LIBERA. *La philosophie médiévale*, PUF, Paris, 1993, pp. XIV and f.
12 Cf. DE LIBERA. "Le relativisme historique." p. 486.
13 Cf. PHILIPP W. ROSEMANN. "La philosophie et ses méthodes de recherche historique réflexions sur la dialectique entre la philosophie et son histoire." in: *Editér, traduire, interpréter. Essais de méthodologie philosophique*, eds. S. G. Lofts, P. W. Rosemann, Peeters, Louvain-Paris, 1997, pp. 2, 12.
14 Cf. There, p. 13; KIJEWSKA. "The history of medieval philosophy." pp. 39–40.
15 Cf. AGNIESZKA KIJEWSKA. "Nicolas de Cues – le philosophe de la Renaissance?" in: *Construction d'un imaginaire collectif européen. De la Renaissance aux Lumières: Allemagne, France, Pologne. Unité et diversité*, ed. L. Kańczugowski, Wydawnictwo KUL, Lublin, 2014, pp. 73–91.
16 Cf. HANS BLUMENBERG. *The Legitimacy of the Modern Age (Studies in Contemporary German Social Thought)*, The MIT Press, Cambridge, MA, 1985, p. 484.

17 Cf. ALEXANDER BIRKENMAJER. *Le rôle joué par les médecins et les naturalistes dans la réception d'Aristote au XII et XIIIe siècle*, Imprimerie Współczesna, Varsovie, 1930.
18 Cf. IRMGARD VON MÜLLER. "Nikolaus von Kues und die Medizin." in: *Nikolaus von Kues 1401-2001. Akten des Symposiums in Bernlastel-Kues von 23. Bis 26. Mai 2001,* eds. K. Kremer, K. Reinhardt, Paulinus Verlag, Trier, 2003, pp. 333–350.
19 Cf. DI I, 12, 33, p. 20: "… to investigate the Maximum symbolically.…"
20 Cf. PETER T. STRUCK. *Birth of the Symbol: Ancient Readers at the Limits of Their Texts,* Princeton University Press, Princeton, 2004, pp. 1–4. Cf. MIKOŁAJ DOMARADZKI. "The Beginnings of Greek Alegoresis." *The Classical World,* 110, n. 3, 2017, p. 301.
21 Cf. BLUMENBERG. *The Legitimacy of the Modern Age*, pp. 490–491.
22 Extending the typically historical approach to the area of economic theology, I have decided to omit references to Cusanus's works in the Latin version and cite them only in the English translation.
23 Cf. PAUL OSLINGTON. "Introduction." in: *The Oxford Handbook of Christianity and Economics,* ed. P. Oslington, Oxford University Press, Oxford, 2014, p. XIII.
24 STEFAN SCHWARZKOPF. "An introduction to economic theology." in: *The Routledge Handbook of Economic Theology,* ed. S. Schwarzkopf, Routledge, London-New York, 2020, p. 1.
25 There, p. 4.
26 Cf. There, pp. 4–5.
27 DEVIN SINGH. *Divine Currency. The Theological Power of Money in the West,* Stanford University Press, Stanford, CA, 2018, pp. 7–8.
28 There, pp. 8–9.
29 SCHWARZKOPF. "An introduction to economic theology." p. 9.
30 There, p. 5; Cf. CARL SCHMIDT. *Political Theology. Four Chapters on the Concept of Sovereignty,* trans. by G. Schwab, The MIT Press, Cambridge MA, London, 1985, p. 36.
31 DOTAN LESHEM. "Oikonomia." in: *The Routledge Handbook of Economic Theology,* ed. S. Schwarzkopf, Routledge, London-New York, 2020, pp. 272–273. Cf. LESHEM. *The Origins of Neoliberalism. Modelling the Economy from Jesus to Foucault,* Columbia University Press, New York, 2016, p. 13.
32 There, pp. 13–14.
33 There, p. 14.
34 Cf. JOHN MONFASANI. "Nicholas of Cusa, the Byzantines and the Greek Language." in: *Greeks and Latins in Renaissance Italy*, Variorum, Ashgate 2004, pp. 220–223.
35 Cf. LESHEM. *The Origins of Neoliberalism,* pp. 15–23.
36 DOUGLAS M. MEEKS. "Economics in the Christian Scriptures." in: *The Oxford Handbook of Christianity and Economics,* ed. P. Oslington, Oxford University Press, Oxford, 2014, pp. 3–21.
37 LESHEM. *The Origins of Neoliberalism*, pp. 25–26.
38 Cf. LESHEM. "Oikonomia." p. 274.
39 There.
40 SCHWARZKOPF. "An introduction to economic theology." p. 1.
41 There, p. 3.
42 ELEONORE STUMP. *Wandering in Darkness. Narrative and the Problem of Suffering,* Oxford University Press, Oxford, 2010, pp. 9–10.
43 Cf. SINGH. *Divine Currency*, p. 6.

44   MARIAN KURDZIAŁEK. "Mediaeval Doctrines of Man as Image of the World." *Roczniki Filozoficzne*, 62, n. 4, 2014, pp. 205–246.
45   Cf. ILARIA L.E. RAMELLI. "The Pastoral Epistles and Hellenistic Philosophy: 1 Timothy 5:1-2, Hierocles, and the 'Contraction of Circles'." *The Catholic Biblical Quarterly*, 73, n. 3, 2011, p. 573.
46   Cf. PIERRE HADOT. *Philosophy as a Way of Life: Spiritual Exercises from Socrates to Foucault,* ed. A. Davidson, trans. by M. Chase, Blackwell, 1995, Malden, MA pp. 81–109.
47   Cf. MARTHA C. NUSSBAUM. *The Therapy of Desire. Theory and Practice in Hellenistic Ethics,* Princeton University Press, Princeton 1994, p. 3.
48   Cf. HADOT. *Philosophy as a Way of Life,* pp. 82–125; cf. ANTONI ŚMIST, *"Łów mądrości" jako ćwiczenie duchowe. Transcendentalno-anagogiczna interpretacja filozofii Mikołaja z Kuzy,* Academicon, Lublin, 2023, pp. 21–30.
49   HADOT. *Philosophy as a Way of Life,* p. 155.
50   PIERRE HADOT. *What is Ancient Philosophy?* trans. by M. Chase, The Belknap Press of Harvard University Press, Cambridge, MA, London, 2004, p. 27.
51   ROWAN WILLIAMS. "Theology as a way of life." in: *The Practice of the Presence of God. Theology as a way of life,* eds. M. Laird, S. T. Hidden, Routledge, London, New York, 2017, p. 13.
52   There, p. 15.

2   The circle of Cusanus's life

Nicholas was born in the year 1401 in Cues, a small town on the Moselle, not far from Trier, into a family of four children. His father, Johann Cryfftz (Krebs), was a rich merchant and shipowner busying himself with the transport of goods and persons on the Moselle and the Rhine; he had extensive trade relations which brought him prosperity and allowed him to possess a magnificent residence on the bank of the Moselle.[1]

It appears that Nicholas, being the eldest son, was expected by his father to take over and continue the trade and position of the head of the family; however, these hopes and expectations came to be disappointed: Nicholas took no interest in his father's occupation, and instead he had a strong liking for serious reading and solitary meditation. Edmond Vansteenberghe quotes a story according to which Nicholas's father, enraged by his son's stubborn refusal to comply with his wishes, pushed the young man from a boat into the water with an oar; in consequence, Nicholas seeking refuge from the paternal wrath found shelter under Prince Manderscheid's protection in Eifel.[2] It is hard to form a judgment as to the truth of this account of the clash between the father and son, although it is a well-established fact that Nicholas was a close friend of the Manderscheid family from very early on in his life. However matters may have stood between the father and son, it is unquestionable that the example of his father's life, dedicated to work, engaged in practical matters and highly economical, was a lasting influence on Nicholas's conduct and the way he managed his own affairs. Meuthen gives the following characterization of Cusanus's style of dealing with practical matters:

> Throughout his life Nicholas of Cusa proved to be a skilful, shrewd, and thrifty businessman. His open attitude toward money, business, and profit did not escape the sharp reproach that this was incompatible with being a member of the clergy. However, this reproach missed the mark in terms of pomp and luxury since

DOI: 10.4324/9781003310693-2

Nicholas was unpretentious and led a simple life. He remained constantly active, engaged in matters both large and small. The distinctive business mentality he inherited shows through everywhere in his life.[3]

Scholars are divided concerning the fact whether Nicholas of Cusa was educated in the famous school of Brothers of the Common Life at Deventer. Edmond Vansteenberghe assumed that he was, but[4] Meuthen resolutely rejects this surmise.[5] The school of Deventer, which especially at the beginning of the 15th century was celebrated for a high level of tuition and an openness to new ideas, counted among its alumni Thomas à Kempis and Denis Ryckel, known as Denis the Carthusian, who accompanied Nicholas of Cusa in his mission in 1451.

In 1416, Nicholas enrolled in the university of Heidelberg, where he began his academic education with the study of liberal arts. The teaching of arts at the faculty of arts at Heidelberg was carried out in the spirit of nominalism, instilled there by Marsilius of Inghen, the first chancellor of that university.[6] The nominalism in question was a position concerning the problem of the nature of universality as it was formulated in the medieval controversies on universals. In opposition to realists, nominalists held that generality or universality cannot be attributed to anything real (essences and ideas); it is instead a distinctive characteristic of signs and in particular of the names of human language (the term 'nominalism' derives from the Latin word *nomen* meaning name). This assumption implied significant theses concerning the structure of reality and the way human mind comes to know it: no universal entities (such as genera, species and essences) really exist; the only things populating the real world are particular beings, individuals, such as Plato or Socrates. It may have been during this initial period of university studies at Heidelberg that Nicholas formed a conviction, which remained unshakable throughout his whole career, that every thing existent in the world is a singular and unique manifestation of the one, supreme, divine archetype. It was this singularist assumption, underlying the whole of Cusanus's thought, that made Ernst Cassirer consider him the father of modern individualism.[7]

However, Nicholas did not stay in Heidelberg for long and it is uncertain whether he gained the title of Bachelor of Arts. In October 1417, we already find him at the University of Padua studying canon and secular law. He attended there to the course by an eminent canonist Prosdocimus de Comitibus (died 1438) in whose house he stayed while he was a student in Padua; another personage he met among his professors was Giuliano Cesarini (1389–1444), soon to become cardinal and Cusanus's friend and collaborator, later the chairman of the Council of Basel. Nicholas at Padua studied legal manuscripts under Cesarini's supervision and later was to dedicate to him three of his significant works: *The Catholic Concordance, On Learned Ignorance* and *On Surmises*.[8]

Also in Padua, Nicholas entered the circle of the pupils of Francis Zabarella (1360–1417), a proponent of conciliarist ecclesiology. The pivotal conception of that theory, based upon insights of Marsilius of Padua, William Ockham, Konrad of Gelnhausen and many others, was the idea of concord (*concordantia*) obtaining between all levels and parts of a structure to be governed, an agreement that is a necessary preliminary condition for the proper functioning of the state and the Church.[9] The idea of universal concord obtaining between diverse parts of a complex structure found ample reflection in Cusanus's work not only in *The Catholic Concordance* and his reformatory activity but also in his theory of the Universe.[10]

Nicholas crowned his studies in Padua in 1423 by earning the title of Doctor of Decrees, that is doctorate of canon law. His six-year period of study in that thriving hub of learning must have contributed significantly to the formation of his mind as well as providing ample and varied nourishment for his intellectual life. Apart from his connections within the legal profession, he met there and formed a lifelong friendship with the outstanding mathematician and astronomer of that time, Paolo Toscanelli (1397–1482); he also came to know in person George of Trebizond, a famous, if highly controversial, Aristotelian and a man of learning, expert in ancient philosophy. The Averroist interpretation of Aristotelian philosophy, the legacy of the 14th-century commentator, John of Jandun, had still many proponents at the philosophical faculty at Padua during Nicholas's sojourn there. He may have attended the lectures of Prosdocimo de Beldomandis, a celebrated astronomer and astrologist of that time. Finally, it was in Padua that he came into contact with two outstanding representatives of the new humanistic learning, the *studia humanitatis*: Guarino da Verona (1374–1460) and Vittorino da Feltre (1378–1446). The intellectual milieu of Padua at that time was a crucible, in which old scholarship and new ideas confronted and fertilized each other and entered into dialectical opposition; undoubtedly, it was fortunate for an open and creative personality like Nicholas's to be there exposed to all these formative influences.[11]

Having completed his studies, he decided to return to his homeland and took the route via Rome, where he heard sermons by the charismatic preacher Bernardino of Siena. Back in Germany, Cusanus attached himself for a short time to the university of Cologne, where he probably lectured on canon law and, more importantly, studied philosophy and theology under the direction of Heimericus de Campo. Possibly, it was on the latter's suggestion that Nicholas acquainted himself with some great masters of the Middle Ages: Pseudo-Dionysius, the masters of the School of Chartres, the Victorines, St. Albert the

Great and, above all, Ramon Lullus.[12] It appears, however, that a purely academic career held no attraction for him since he twice, in 1428 and 1435, turned down an offer by the university of Leuven of a chair of canon law. Instead, he chose a life of affairs and soon gained a reputation as an efficient canonist lawyer; about 1426, he came to be employed as a secretary by the then archbishop of Trier, Otto of Ziegenhain. For the numerous tasks he performed for the archbishop, he was rewarded with benefices. Collecting benefices as a means of personal enrichment was a widespread and often denounced vice of the clergy and other Church functionaries in Cusanus's days, yet he himself appears to have successfully resisted to this kind of enticement and to have considered his rewards as so many new responsibilities rather than occasions for personal gain. Erich Meuthen thus characterized the dilemmas facing Nicholas and his attitude toward the worldly and material aspect of his position:

> For these clergy the church was not acquainted with any other system than the political organization of the day in which people were compensated not with civil service wages, but with fiefs and benefices – that is, with material goods. This method naturally suggested itself for the administration of the church, though an alternative would have been for the church, in accordance with the demands of the poverty movement, to assume an absolutely spiritual form. It is true that in his correspondence Nicholas of Cusa posed as clearly as he could the question about renouncing earthly goods, but he balanced this with the counter-question whether withdrawal from the world might mean withdrawal from responsibility for the world. He decided in favor of engagement with the world. However, then the task arises to decide how much of the income should go for personal use, how much for the material support of the institution, and, finally, how much for the response to the evangelical call for charity. Conclusions about Cusanus's simple way of life free him from any suspicion of enriching himself personally.[13]

The period in the service of the archbishop of Trier proved very fruitful for Nicholas and brought him new interests and friendships. As the archbishop's secretary he had easy access to episcopal and monastic archives and libraries and his researches brought to light a number of important legal documents from the epoch of Charlemagne and even earlier. This provided him with sufficient evidence to prove that the famous Donation of Constantine, which purported to be a decree issued by the emperor Constantine the Great and on which papal claims to the temporal authority over the western part of the Roman Empire rested, was an 8th-century production, a discovery later strengthened with philological arguments and published by Lorenzo Valla in his celebrated *Declamation*.[14] This and other archival finds earned Nicholas both opponents and supporters, the latter mostly among Italian humanists, such as the Vatican librarian Poggio Bracciolini, who keenly sought after manuscripts containing works handed down from classical antiquity.[15]

When in 1430 Cusanus's employer, the archbishop Otto of Trier, died, Nicholas found himself drawn into the controversy around the succession to that ancient see, which was all the more heated as its incumbent was one of the Princes entitled to elect the emperor of the Holy Roman Empire[16]. The chapter of the diocese of Trier designated two candidates for that office: one Jakob of Sierck and the other Ulrich of Manderscheid, dean of the chapter of Cologne. Meanwhile the pope Martin V designated Raban of Helmstadt for the archiepiscopal office of Trier. Naturally enough, this resulted in a dispute between Ulrich and the pope, Nicholas participating in it on the side of the former as his secretary and legal adviser. It was an associate of Ulrich that he appeared in 1432 at the Council of Basel and soon succeeded in winning the recognition of the council fathers for his expertise as a canonist and a capacity for hard work. Although on 15 May 1434 the council gave their support to the papal candidate for the archbishopric of Trier, Nicholas had already become a member of a number of conciliar commissions.[17] He was first appointed to the Commission on Matters of Faith, and his activity as a member of that team bore fruit in the shape of two works: *The Catholic Concordance* of 1433 and *On Presidential Authority in a General Council*. While the former established his position among the conciliarists of the Council, the latter sought a way of reconciliation between the supporters and opponents of the pope.[18]

Another commission in the works of which he participated was the one appointed to deal with the matters concerning the Hussites. In 1433, Nicholas wrote *Communion under Both Kinds*, a treatise which contained a statement of his position concerning Utraquists. He also took part in the work on the improvement of the system of time reckoning and presented his suggestions in the document *Reform of the Calendar*. Erich Meuthen observed concerning this work and the later treatise *Conjecture on the Last Days* that they show "how closely Nicholas was able to connect mathematical and astronomical seriousness with prognosticating number play that was a child of its time."[19]

Nicholas's commitment to the interests of Ulrich of Manderscheid exposed him to a threat of excommunication, and his activity as a theorist of conciliarism highlighted even further the rift between himself and the Roman Curia. Meanwhile, in the year 1435, the collegiate chapter of the diocese of Münstermaifeld, not far from Koblenz, elected him parish-priest of St. Martin and Sever; Nicholas had to wait a year for the papal confirmation of that benefice.[20] The fact that he finally obtained it may be indicative of a dissension having gradually arisen between himself and the camp of the confirmed conciliarists. This disagreement came to a head when the council fathers failed to reach an agreement on the venue of the projected ecumenical council that would bring together delegates from the Greek and Latin Churches and, it was hoped for, end the long-standing schism between the two branches of Christianity. In this question, Nicholas refused to side with hard-core conciliarists, and in May 1437, he left Basel for Ferrara, to which pope Eugene IV convoked a new council in January 1438. This act was significant in that it represented a definitive breach of Cusanus's alliance with the conciliarist movement and his transition to the papal position. Shortly before this decisive move, possibly in 1436, Nicholas was ordained priest. His quality as an intellectual, canonist and diplomat was duly appreciated by his superiors, and yet in the same year 1437, he was appointed member of the pontifical delegation, which was sent to Constantinople to bring the Emperor Joannes VIII Palaeologus and the representatives of the hierarchy of the Greek Church to the projected ecumenical council. Meuthen comments on Cusanus's journey as follows: "He brought back from Constantinople a Greek manuscript that contained the sixth to eighth councils."[21] These manuscripts containing the documents of Greek councils were to be used in preparatory negotiations to open the way for the reunification of the two churches.[22] Other Greek texts Cusanus brought home from his voyage to Constantinople included Proclus's *Platonic Theology* and works by the Greek Church Fathers. In Greece, he also met and made friends with intellectually and politically important persons, such as the metropolitan of Nicaea Bessarion, a humanist and neoplatonist scholar, translator of Aristotle's *Metaphysics* into Latin, later to be made cardinal of the Roman Catholic Church, and the famous, if unorthodox, neoplatonist, Georgios Gemistos Plethon.[23]

The Latin mission to Constantinople lasted from 27 November 1437 to 8 February 1438. On his voyage back from Constantinople, Nicholas had a peculiar experience, a kind of divine illumination, which profoundly influenced his way of thinking. He mentioned this experience in the dedicatory letter to Cardinal Giuliano Cesarini, which he added to his treatise *On Learned Ignorance* finished in 1440. This experience is usually seen as being the turning point in Cusanus's life, awaking him to the life of mystical contemplation. It was not that he abandoned his engagement in the affairs of the Church, but from that moment on, he tried to combine his *vita activa*, an active participation in the running of the Church, with *vita contemplativa*, a disinterested vision of the ultimate truth. This is how he himself refers to his experience in the often quoted passage from the dedicatory letter to his protector and friend:

> Receive now, Reverend Father, the things which I have long desired to attain by various doctrinal-approaches but could not – until, while I was at sea en route back from Greece, I was led (by, as I believe, a heavenly gift from the Father of lights, from whom comes every excellent gift) to embrace – in learned ignorance and through a transcending of the incorruptible truths which are humanly knowable – incomprehensible things incomprehensibly. Thanks to Him who is Truth, I have now expounded this [learned ignorance] in these books, which [since they proceed] from [one and] the same principle, can be condensed or expanded.[24]

Nicholas took part in the initial sessions of the Council of Ferrara, which later relocated to Florence, yet it was not his destiny to play a major role in this assembly: another task assigned him by the pope claimed his active presence elsewhere, and notably in his native land of Germany. The clash between conciliarists and defenders of papal supremacy remained unresolved, with the fathers of the rump council of Basel stubbornly continuing to oppose Pope Eugene IV. In Germany, most of the politically significant actors adopted neutrality on the issue, encouraged in this by Albert II Habsburg, who was elected in 1438 as the successor of the deceased Emperor Sigismund. In this continuing controversy over the supreme authority in the Church, the pope thought it vital to enlist the support of the powerful German Princes. With this in view, he decided to send a mission to German lands that would try to win the local rulers there over to his cause.[25] Cusanus was selected for that embassy, being the only German on that mission. His commitment to the papal cause was so whole-hearted, and his activity in performing the allotted task so strenuous, that his contemporary Aeneas Silvius Piccolomini, later to become Pope Pius II, called him "Hercules of the Eugenians." Erich Meuthen sums up as follows Cusanus's occupations during the decade 1438–1448 spent as a papal envoy in his native land:

> During the ten years Nicholas spent in Germany as papal legate he was occupied with numerous affairs of his homeland. In some cases there were ecclesiastical tasks that the pope or legates entrusted to him, among which the work of reform was prominent. In other case he was approached by the nobility, middle-class citizens, prelates, foundations, corporations, and institutions of his homeland to mediate their disputes. Just to enumerate all these activities would fil many pages![26]

As there was no watertight barrier between politics and religion in those days and the two often merged into one, Cusanus's diplomatic activity was always closely related to his activity as spiritual reformer. It appears that the efforts of the Eugenian envoys in Germany after 1438 brought appreciable results. The new King of Germany after Albert II's death in 1439, Frederick of the House of Habsburg, later to become Holy Roman Emperor as Frederick III, after much diplomatic maneuvering signed on 17 February 1448 in Vienna a concordat with the Holy See. Tommaso Parentucelli, since 1447 Pope Nicholas V, Cusanus's former colleague on the German embassy and eyewitness of the latter's strenuous engagement, in recognition of his contribution to the success, created him cardinal on 20 December 1448 and assigned him St. Peter in Chains as his titular church.[27] In March 1450, the Cardinal of St. Peter in Chains was made bishop of the diocese of Brixen (Bressanone) in South Tyrol by pope Nicholas, the position which entailed the title and dignity of a Prince of the Holy Roman Empire. However, he could only take the government of the diocese which was entrusted to him with a delay caused by a new and unprecedented task set him by the pope. The year 1450 was proclaimed a Jubilee year, and the pope wished that the spiritual gifts of the Jubilee should be made available not only to those who would come on a pilgrimage to Rome but also to those who would not be able to undertake such a long and arduous journey; therefore, he sent Cusanus once again to Germany as his legate to travel around the land, preach the Jubilee and dispense the indulgences.[28] His legacy involved attempts to undertake reform in various areas of religious and social life in Germany. This reformatory zeal, which later on also inspired the governance of his diocese of Brixen, earned him as many supporters as fierce opponents and is a very uncommon phenomenon in his epoch.

It was as late as before Easter 1452 that Nicholas finally came to Brixen to assume the spiritual care of the flock entrusted to himself yet was not given a benevolent reception there. The reason for this cold welcome was the fact that the local chapter had proposed another candidate for the bishop of the place, namely Leonhard Wiesmayer, chancellor of the Archduke Sigismund Habsburg and nephew of Emperor Frederick III, so the pope's overruling this choice was resented as an encroachment upon the local freedom and Cusanus regarded as an intruder imposed by a high handed and unsympathetic authority. As Brian Pavlac has shown, the period of Nicholas' activity as bishop of Brixen has given rise to most contradictory assessments by Cusanus's students: "...historians generally agree about the events of Cusanus's episcopal tenure, but disagree sharply when trying to divine the motivations or significance of them."[29]

As bishop of Brixen, Nicholas continued his commitment to the program of reform and strove "to make his see an exemplary diocese."[30] He undertook a reform of the diocesan administration paying attention in particular to the management of the diocesan finances; he also searched through the local archives and unearthed some forgotten documents, on the authority of which he tried to reclaim the landed property once forcibly taken away from the local church institutions. However, the result of this vigorous action was the open war with the local overlord, Duke Sigismund of Austria of the House of Habsburg, who found support among some part of the diocesan clergy, unfavorably disposed to Cusanus's reforms. In June 1457, Sigismund invited Nicholas to the abbey of Wilten close to Innsbruck, yet Nicholas, fearing a conspiracy on the part of the Duke, left Wilten and took residence in the castle of Andraz, close to the Italian border and thus providing an easy way of escape in case the Duke should undertake some violent moves against him. From Andraz, Cusanus attempted to exert some pressure upon his Princely opponent.[31] In September 1458, he left for Rome, summoned there by the newly elected pope, his one-time friend Enea Silvio Piccolomini, now Pope Pius II. During the protracted absence of the Prince-bishop, Duke Sigismund so much strengthened his position in the local politics such that when Cusanus attempted to come back to his see in the early 1460, Sigismund was able to make the return impossible for him. The Prince-bishop then took refuge in a small town of Bruneck, which the duke put under siege, finally taking it on Easter Sunday, according to the memoirs of Pius II.[32] Nicholas, fearing a massacre of the defenders loyal to himself, gave up his last defense, the castle of the town. When taken into custody by the duke, he promised not to seek redress for the violence he fell victim to; however, when returned his freedom, Cardinal of St. Peter in Chains took back his promise saying, that made under coercion it had no binding power. Nevertheless, from his clash with Duke Sigismund, he came out the loser: after 1460, he never returned to his diocese of Brixen. The last period of his life was spent in the close surroundings of Pope Pius II as his aide and trusted advisor, who did not shrink from openly criticizing some of the pontiff's ideas, if he thought it appropriate.[33]

The pope, wishing to take full advantage of Cusanus's experience, appointed him a member of a commission working on a reform of the Roman Curia; Nicholas, in compliance with the pope's wishes, prepared an outline of the bull *Reformatio generalis*, in which he suggested a number of new regulations, among others a ban on cumulation of ecclesiastical offices and a stricter and more efficient control of provincial Church institution by Rome. Pius II included some of Cusanus's suggestions in the project of a bull he planned to issue in 1464 and entitle *Pastor aeternus*.[34]

Cusanus characteristically preferred peaceful to war solutions, and, accordingly, he adopted a reserved attitude to the idea of an armed crusade against the Turks, who in 1453 took Constantinople. Yet Pius II, who shared the traditional belief of the medieval papacy that a crusade was a legitimate means of solving political problems arising on the borders of Christendom as well as an expedient to end the perennial quarrels among the Catholic Princes and unite them for a common purpose, convoked in 1459 a congress to Mantua to start preparations for a military expedition of all Catholic leaders against the threatening Ottoman empire. Undiscouraged by the failure of the congress, the pope continued efforts to mobilize as much of Christian forces as he could against the Ottomans. He called on his friend and adviser, Cusanus, to assist him in his endeavors, and in summer 1464, he summoned him to Ancona, where the pope intended to come to lead the projected crusade in person. Although Nicholas since 1461 had been gradually withdrawing from active involvement in ecclesiastical politics, he set out for Ancona in compliance with the call but never arrived there: he died on the way in Todi, on 11 August 1464. Cusanus was interred in his titular Roman church of St. Peter in Chains, while his heart, according to his wish, was brought to his native Kues and deposed in St. Nicholas chapel of the hospital he himself founded and endowed.

Notes

1   ERICH MEUTHEN. *Nicholas of Cusa. A Sketch for a Biography,* trans. by D. Crowner, G. Christianson, The Catholic University of America Press, Washington D.C., 2010, p. 10. Cf. Donald F. DUCLOW. "Life and Works." in: *Introducing Nicholas of Cusa. A Guide to a Renaissance Man,* eds. Ch. M. Bellito, Th. M. Izbicki, G. Christianson, Paulist Press, New York-Mahwah, NJ, 2004, pp. 25–26.
2   Cf. EDMOND VANSTEENBERGHE. *Le cardinal Nicolas de Cues,* Paris, 1920 (repr. Frankfurt am Main, 1963), pp. 5–6.
3   MEUTHEN. *Nicholas of Cusa,* p. 11.
4   Cf. VANSTEENBERGHE. *Le cardinal Nicolas de Cues,* pp. 7–8.
5   Cf. MEUTHEN. *Nicholas of Cusa,* p. 12; cf. PAUL E. SIGMUND. *Nicholas of Cusa and Medieval Political Thought,* Harvard University Press, Cambridge, MA, 1963, p. 21.
6   Cf. MEUTHEN. *Nicholas of Cusa,* p. 15. Cf. *Nicholas of Cusa – A Companion to his Life and his Times.* ed. M. Watanabe, G. Christianson, Th. Izbicki, Ashgate, Burlington, 2011, pp. 235–237.
7   Cf. ERNST CASSIRER. *The Individual and the Cosmos in Renaissance Philosophy,* trans. by M. Domandi, Dover Publications, INC., Mineola, New York, 2000, p. 37.
8   Cf. *Nicholas of Cusa – A Companion,* pp.100–103, 239; cf. SIGMUND. *Nicholas of Cusa,* p. 24.
9   Cf. There, pp. 22–26; MEUTHEN. *Nicholas of Cusa,* pp. 17–18; cf. THOMAS E. MORRISSEY. "The Political Philosophy of Franciscus Zabarella as Seen in His Public Addresses and Other Works." in: *Nicholas of Cusa and Times of Transition. Essays in Honor of Gerald Christianson,* eds. Th. M. Izbicki, J. Aleksander, D. F. Duclow, Brill, Leiden-Boston, 2019, p. 16.
10 Cf. CC I, 4, p. 5.

11 Cf. MEUTHEN. *Nicholas of Cusa*, p. 19; cf. M. WATANABE. "Political and Legal Ideas." in: *Nicholas of Cusa. A Guide*, pp. 143–144; VAN-STEENBERGHE. *Le cardinal Nicolas de Cues*, pp. 10–12, 19–24; JULIE K. TANAKA. "From universal to local: German Identity in Nicholas of Cusa's Catholic Concordance." *Renaissance Studies*, 36, n. 2, 2021, p. 299.

12 Cf. *Nicholas of Cusa – A Companion*, pp. 94–96; cf. MEUTHEN. *Nicholas of Cusa*, pp. 30–32; cf. SIGMUND. *Nicholas of Cusa*, pp. 25–26.

13 MEUTIIEN. *Nicholas of Cusa*, pp. 22–23.

14 Cf. There, p. 28. Cf. PAULINE M. WATTS. "Renaissance Humanism." in: *Introducing Nicholas of Cusa. A Guide to a Renaissance Man*, eds. Ch. M. Bellito, Th. M. Izbicki, G. Christianson, Paulist Press, New York-Mahwah, NJ, 2004, p. 174; cf. CC III, II, 294–295 pp. 217.

15 SIGMUND. *Nicholas of Cusa*, p. 28; cf. MEUTHEN. *Nicholas of Cusa*, pp. 33–35.

16 Cf. SIGMUND. "Introduction." in: *Nicholas of Cusa, The Catholic Concordance*, ed. P. E. Sigmund, Cambridge University Press, Cambridge, 1991, pp. XII–XV.

17 Cf. MEUTHEN. *Nicholas of Cusa*, pp. 35–38.

18 Cf. There, pp. 38–42; Cf. SIGMUNT. *Nicholas of Cusa*, p. 219.

19 MEUTHEN. *Nicholas of Cusa*, p. 41.

20 Cf. There, p. 52; cf. *Nicholas of Cusa – A Companion*, p. 263.

21 MEUTHEN. *Nicholas of Cusa*, p. 53.

22 Cf. H. LAWRENCE BOND. "Nicholas of Cusa from Constantinople to *Learned Ignorance:* The Historical Matrix for the formation of *De docta ignorantia.*" in: *Reform, Representation and theology in Nicholas of Cusa and his age*, eds. H. L. Bond, G. Christianson, Routledge, London, New York, 2011, pp. 201–204.

23 MEUTHEN, *Nicholas of Cusa*, pp. 54–56.

24 DI. *Letter*, 263, p. 151; cf. MEUTHEN. *Nicholas of Cusa*, p. 68.

25 Cf. There, p. 69.

26 There, p. 72.

27 Cf. There, p. 80.

28 There, p. 88.

29 BRIAN A. PAVLAC. "Nicolaus Cusanus as Prince-Bishop of Brixen (1450-1464): Historians and a Conflict of Church and State." *Historical Reflections*, 21, n. 1, 1995, p. 133.

30 There, p. 136.

31 Cf. *Nicholas of Cusa – A Companion*, pp. 349–351; PAVLAC. "Nicolaus Cusanus as Prince." pp. 137–138.

32 Cf. Pius II. *Pamiętniki* IV, ed. A. von Heck, trans. by J. Wojtkowski, Biblioteca Apostolica Vaticana, Marki, 2005, p. 205.

33 Cf. There, VIII, 9, p. 363. Cf. EMILY O'BRIEN. *The "Commentaries" of Pope Pius II (145801464) and the Crisis of the Fifteenth-Century Papacy*, University of Toronto Press, Toronto, Buffalo, London, 2015, pp. 139–141.

34 Cf. There, p. 80.

3 The circle of Cusanus's literary activity

There are three spheres in Cusanus's life and career that are so intertwined with one another that it is difficult to isolate one of them for discussion and leave aside the other two; these are the events of his life, his activity as a writer and his indefatigable efforts to carry out reform of the ecclesiastical and social structures around himself. The same can be said about his literary output, in which different areas of concern interpenetrate and elucidate one another. Jovino de Guzman Miroy aptly observed,

> Cusanus was neither merely political nor speculative nor the combination of the two. One would be misrepresenting him were he to read Cusanus' political works while oblivious to his speculative thought or were he to take him for a reclusive mystic despite his political embroilments.[1]

When one refers to Cusanus as a mystic, what is usually alluded to is Nicholas's celebrated illumination experienced on a ship travelling from Constantinople in 1437/1438 and described in the dedicatory letter to Cesarini appended to his *On Learned Ignorance*. Another such illuminative experience is mentioned as having taken place on Easter 1464 and left Nicholas with a deeper comprehension of the Supreme Principle.[2] More cautious students of his life and output, such as M. Boyle, are rather inclined to see in the descriptions of these enlightenments a literary *topos* rather than reports on some facts concerning inner life.[3] Nevertheless, it is a fact that the experience of 1437/1438 opened a new chapter in Nicholas's life and inspired a long series of works on speculative and spiritual topics. The period of nearly two and a half decades of his literary activity concerned with the First Principle, and the ways it lends itself to human contemplation have been divided by Cusanus's scholars into various phases, giving rise to the question whether his long literary career allows us to discern a certain evolution in his views and the way he presented them. The answer to this question seems far from

DOI: 10.4324/9781003310693-3

straightforward, especially in the light of Cusanus's own self-assessment in one of his last works, *Compendium* of 1463:

> You now know the thoughts that I have elsewhere more extensively expressed about these topics, in many and various works, which you can read subsequently to this *Compendium*. And you will find that the First Beginning, who is everywhere the same, has appeared to us in various ways and that I have portrayed in various ways His various manifestations.[4]

To take this declaration at its face value, one would conclude that throughout his whole career, Nicholas was concerned with only one subject: the First Principle, and yet there are good reasons to distinguish different approaches in his treatment of his arch-concern, which appeared at various stages of his creative period.

It is good to begin an overview of Nicholas's recorded literary output with his *Catholic Concordance* of 1433. This work is the ripe fruit of his intense participation in the debates of the first years of the Council of Basel; it is usually interpreted as a voice of vigorous support of conciliar ideology. Yet the strong pro-conciliar bias of this work contrasts very strongly with Cusanus's later engagement on the side of successive popes and also sheds light on the nature of the illuminative experience on the sea as a turning point in his life. It is probably significant that after his break with the conciliarists of Basel he never returned to the discussion of the problems of ecclesiastical politics and omitted *The Catholic Concordance* from the collective edition of his works he prepared at the end of his life.

In short, it has been customary to distinguish in Nicholas's literary career three phases or periods. The early period, from the start in 1433 to 1438, brought a series of scripts on matters of ecclesiology, canon law and ecclesiastical politics: *The Catholic Concordance, On the Authority of the President in a General Council* and *Reform of a calendar.*

The middle period of Cusanus's literary activity is inaugurated by his most famous treatise, namely *On Learned Ignorance* of 1440, which was inspired by his "experience on the sea." This work is the first in the long series of writings concerned with the First Principle and the way human mind can know it and express its knowledge. The author states tersely:

> I have endeavored, for purpose of investigating this pathway, to explain [matters] to those of ordinary intelligence as clearly as I could. Avoiding all roughness of style. I show at the outset that learned ignorance has its basis in the fact that the precise truth is inapprehensible.[5]

As Edward Cranz has observed, typical of Cusanus's works of this period is (1) a very strongly accentuated tension between the conception of God, who is conceived, in accordance with the tradition coming from St. Anselm, as the maximal being and the being of creations, which come from and completely depend on God for their existence.[6]

This Maximum or Supreme Being is, as Pseudo-Dionysius never tired of emphasizing, the highest Unity, which, on account of its simplicity remains forever inaccessible and incomprehensible to the intellect.[7] The intellectual knowledge may progress toward the all-comprehensive unity of the absolute truth, but it can never attain to it and remains forever shut in the sphere of verisimilitude. This novel conception of intellectual knowledge, forever striving for more and always short of its ultimate goal, is expounded in the work *On Surmises* (*De coniecturis*) of 1442–1443.[8] God's radical and unbridgeable transcendence is discussed at length in the dialogue *On the Hidden God* (*De Deo abscondito*) of the early 1445; the discussion is continued in *On seeking God* (*De quaerendo Deum*) and in *On being a son of God* (*De filiatione Dei*) of the same 1445. The year 1446 brought *The gift of the Father of Lights* (*De dato Patris luminum*), the title referring to the often quoted verse from St. James's Epistle (1, 17f.), which Cusanus also quoted in his letter to Cardinal Cesarini appended to *On Learned Ignorance*. In the same year, Nicholas produced *A Surmise about the Last Days* (*Coniectura de ultimis diebus*) and in 1447 *Dialogue on the Genesis* (*Dialogus de genesi*). In the year 1449, Nicholas penned *A defence of Learned Ignorance* (*Apologia doctae ignorantiae*), a response to the objections to Cusanus's ideas put forward by John Wenck in his polemic entitled *On unknown learning* (*De ignota litteratura*).

Another characteristic feature of the works of the middle period according to Edward Cranz is (2) the absence of distinction between the spheres of the cognitive operations of reason and intellect; the former restricted to the realm of apparent non-contradiction, and the latter is capable of grasping the reality behind apparent contradictions.[9] These two modes of knowing by the human mind and the corresponding respective objective spheres would only be clearly distinguished in the last work of Cusanus's middle period, namely in *The Vision of God* (*De visione Dei*), preceded and prepared by a trilogy of dialogues of 1450 devoted to epistemological questions, namely *The Layman on Wisdom* (*Idiota de Sapientia*), *The Layman on Mind* (*Idiota de mente*) and *The Layman on Experiments Done with Weight-scales* (*Idiota de staticis experimentis*). In these dialogues, (3) Cusanus would not only represent his ideas as a continuation of the main philosophical traditions originating with Plato and Aristotle but also take up some motifs deriving from Christian Socratism in the spirit of Francis Petrarch.[10]

Another feature of Cusanus's productions of the middle period is (4) the extensive use of the symbolism of darkness in referring to God's proper inaccessibility to human knowing, being the consequence of His ontological and epistemological transcendence. References to obscurity and darkness accompany his descriptions of the human cognitive approach to God. For instance in *On Learned Ignorance*, he writes as follows:

> Therefore, we who are believers in Christ are led in learned ignorance unto the Mountain that is Christ and that we are forbidden to touch with the nature of our animality. When we attempt to view this Mountain with our intellectual eye, we fall into an obscuring mist, knowing that within this mist is the Mountain on which, alone, all living beings possessed of an intellect are well pleased to dwell.[11]

In *A Defence of Learned Ignorance*, undoubtedly galled by the widespread incomprehension of his position and ideas, he expresses a conviction that some kind of literature, namely that treating of sublime and mysterious matters, should only be allowed to readers with a proper intellectual background and suitable preparation.[12]

The third and last phase in Nicholas's literary activity opens the treatise *On Eyeglasses (De beryllo)* of 1458. The beryl he considers forms a kind of lens as used in eyeglasses and thus an illustration of union of opposites, being both concave and convex, its transparency allowing to see all things beyond, as it were, the sphere of contradiction. In this way, a beryl is an illustration of how, through union of opposites, we can arrive at an immediate intellectual vision of God as the Absolute Principle.

With this work, (1) Cusanus introduces the theme of intentionality into the consideration of the relationship between the Creator and the creation: the latter is the result of the intention (*intentio*) of Divine Will:

> Now, things-that-are-made-voluntarily exist insofar as they are conformed to the [creating] will, and so their form is the intention of their commander. Now, an intention is a likeness of the intender – a likeness which is communicable to, and receivable by, another. Therefore, every creature is and intention of the Omnipotent Will.[13]

With regard to God, (2) Cusanus goes beyond the language of being and attempts to apply new and specially meaningful names to God: Light and Equality in the text of *On Equality (De aequalitate)* of 1459, Beginning in *On the Beginning (De principio)* of the same year and his own coinage *Possest*, as in the dialogue *De possest* of 1460. The vocable *Possest* is a contraction of two Latin words – *posse* and *est* – and is a meaningful name in indicating that in God every possibility regarding Himself is actuality; that is, whatever it is possible for Him to be, He actually is. In the years 1461–1462, he composes *On Non-Other (De Non-Aliud)*, in which the description of God as Not-other serves to highlight the absolute incommensurability of God with regard to all human intellectual insights.

In his last work, composed in 1464, the year of his death, *Concerning the Loftiest Level of Contemplative Reflection* (*De apice theoriae*), Cusanus attributed to God the name *Posse Ipsum*: pure or absolute possibility. In the work of 1462 *On the Pursuit of Wisdom* (*De venatione sapientiae*), God is given the name of Wisdom, and in the *Game of Spheres* (*De ludo globi*) composed in 1462–1463, the name of Mind. The last two names indicate the cognitive relationship of man to God as Mind and Wisdom: of all material creatures, only man can read off God's intention. In the works of that period, Nicholas (3) expressly distinguishes between the cognitive spheres of intellect or intelligence, the intellectual cognitive power, whose function is to reach beyond that "wall of Paradise," which is unity of opposites[14] and of ordinary human reason, bound to the domain of non-contradictory concepts. For instance in *On Eyeglasses*, he draws a distinction between three kinds of knowing: "perceptual, intellectual and intelligential."[15] This distinction between these three kinds of knowledge Cusanus attributes to the thought of Saint Augustine, although reference here is also made to Boethius and the reception of his writings in the school of Chartres. In the works of his final period, Nicholas often quotes representatives of the medieval philosophical tradition (4); this is in particular noticeable in *On the Pursuit of Wisdom* and in *Compendium* of 1463.[16] He still remains in the sphere of influence of Pseudo-Dionysius and the latter's symbolism, yet there is a marked shift in his last works toward the symbolism of light and away from the language of darkness and obscurity. This is particularly noticeable in his last treatise *Concerning the Loftiest Level of Contemplative Reflection*:

> Therefore, Possibility itself is called *Light* by some saints – not perceptible light or rational light or intelligible light but the Light of all things that can give light – since nothing can possibly be brighter or clearer ore more beautiful than Possibility. Therefore, look unto perceptible light, without which there cannot be perceptual seeing.[17]

Regardless of whether his whole productive literary activity is interpreted in terms of development or evolution, or, as he himself suggested in *Compendium*, as constant reiteration, be it in different form, of one and the same message, the unquestionable truth with regard to it is that all his works are so many examples of *manuductio*, attempts to lead the reader, by the hand, as it were, to ever more complete discovery and comprehension of the Absolute First Principle: reading Cusanus is like undergoing intellectual initiation, a preparation for enlightenment concerning the nature of the Supreme Reality.

The same tendency to lead the listener to progressive illumination is also present in his sermons, which, parenetic by their nature, share many topic and interests with his philosophical and theological treatises. During his long activity as a preacher, Cusanus delivered many hundred sermons, of which many were recorded in writing; to our days 293 survive, which accounts for about one third of his total output.[18] His activity as a predicator can be divided into periods roughly corresponding to the phases of his philosophico-theological productivity and firmly rooted in the circumstances of his biography. The first period includes sermons I-LXXV delivered between 1430, the year he was elected dean of the chapter of St. Florian in Koblenz and 1449, the year immediately preceding his Jubilee tour in Germany. This first period can be further subdivided into two phases, according to the circumstances of his biography: 1430–1439 (Cusanus's active involvement in the activities of the Councils of Basel and Ferrara) and 1439–1449 (his legacy in Germany on behalf of Pope Eugene IV). The second period, from 1450 to 1458, includes his mission in Germany as a Holy Jubilee preacher and his activity as bishop of Brixen. The third and last period of Cusanus's predicatory activity covers the years 1459–1463, when he was a member of the papal court as an adviser of Pope Pius II. Most of the sermons delivered by Nicholas were preached in vernacular German, but their records, often very cursory, were made and survive in Latin. Many concerns and interests found in Cusanus's sermons closely correspond to the leading concerns of his treatises.

In Cusanus's literary legacy, there are two more strands of interests, which, although secondary to his main theological and philosophical preoccupations, nevertheless were significant in helping to form his ideas on these and the way he discussed them. One such current of interest concerns broadly conceived mathematics. Nicholas viewed all human cognition in terms of approaching the truth rather than grasping it with precision; among all fields of human knowing, he specially valued mathematical knowledge as characterized by the highest degree of precision and clarity humanly accessible. Nevertheless, as Tamara Albertini rightly observed, he himself was no professional mathematician and his discussions of geometrical figures and other mathematical notions mainly served the purpose of illustration and visualization of philosophical matters.[19]

Jean-Marie Nicolle, the critical editor of Cusanus's mathematical writings, is even more dismissive of the value of his contribution to mathematical sciences in his terse statement that all mathematical researches of Nicholas of Cusa end in a failure.[20] This is in particular true of his treatises about the problem of squaring the circle, which was close to his mind as an example illustrating the principle of unity of opposites. Still, he cannot be simply dismissed as a dilettante in mathematics: the conclusions following from his philosophical considerations illustrated with mathematical examples had an impact on scientific research in the subsequent centuries and undoubtedly contributed to the transformation of the scientific representation of the Universe achieved in early modern times, a topic to which we will yet return.

The other subsidiary strand in Nicholas's concerns is the interest he took in other religions, in particular his discussion with Islam. During the sessions of the council of Basel, Nicholas got in touch with John of Segovia, a professor at the University of Salamanca, with whom he discussed the problem of the relationship between Christianity and other religions; at that time, he also obtained a copy of the 12th-century translation of the Koran by Robert of Ketton and some other texts translated from Arabic, the so-called Toledan documents ascribed to the translator John of Seville.[21]

Cusanus was prompted to take up the study of Islam by the political context of his days, Europe being increasingly threatened by the powerful Ottoman Empire, and in particular by the dramatic event of the fall of Constantinople to the invading Turks in 1453. Precisely in this year, Cusanus wrote a remarkable work entitled *On Peaceful Unity of Faith* (*De pace fidei*). In this work, Cusanus represents a vision of a heavenly court presided over by an Almighty King, whose Word gathers representatives of diverse nations and religions before the throne of God for discussion of the most important points of disagreement between various systems of religious faith. The debate is directed by the principle formulated by the Word:

> Therefore, for all those who are of sound understanding there is one religion and worship, which is presupposed in all the diversity of rites.[22]

It is worthwhile here to quote the comment of Michel de Certeau on that work, which he described as follows:

> ...an anti-Babelian "vision" of a heavenly "theatre" in which, one after another, a delegate from each nation gets up to bear witness to the movement which supports it. Greek, Italian, Arab, Indian, Chaldean, Jeu, Scythian, Gaul, Persian, Syrian, Turk, Spaniard, German, Tartar, Armenian, and so forth, each one comes to attest in the language of his own tradition to the truth which is one: the harmony of "free spirits" answer the furies of fanaticism.[23]

Cusanus returned to the discussion with Islam in 1461 when he wrote a work for Pius II entitled *A Scrutiny of the Koran* (*Cribratio Alkorani*). Possibly some inspiration for this study came to him from Denis the

Carthusian, who dedicated to himself his treatise *Against Muhammad's Perfidy* (*Contra perfidiam Mahometi*). A manuscript containing Denis's work with notes by Nicholas's own hand is still preserved in Kues in the library of the Cusanusstift.[24] Cusanus's *Scrutiny* strives to show that the teaching of the Koran is implicitly trinitarian and Christological and that Prophet Muhammad himself purposely concealed some elevated truths from the ignorant.[25]

Interestingly, a position based on similar assumptions is found in *Letter to Muhammad* dispatched by Pope Pius II to Sultan Muhammad II in 1461, in which the pope exhorted the ruler to embrace Christianity and accept baptism. Possibly, this extraordinary attempt by a pope to win a convert at the highest level of political authority and thus bring about the end of the hostility between two great religious systems owed its inspiration to the ideas developed by Nicholas in his *Scrutiny of the Koran*.[26]

Notes

1 JOVINO de GUZMAN MIROY. *Tracing Nicholas of Cusa's Early Development. The Relationship between "De concordantial catholica "and "De docta ignorantia."* Peeters, Leuven- Louvain-la-Neuve, 2009, p. 44.
2 Cf. H. LAURENCE BOND. "Mystical Theology," in: *Introducing Nicholas of Cusa. A Guide to a Renaissance Man*, eds. Ch. M. Bellitto, Th. M. Izbicki, G. Christianson, Paulist Press, New York-Mahwah, NJ, 2004, pp. 205–209, 219–224. Cf. AT 2, p. 1423.
3 Cf. MARJORIE O'ROURKE BOYLE. "Cusanus at Sea: The Topicality of Illuminative Discourse," *The Journal of Religion*, 71, n. 2, 1991, pp. 180–210.
4 C 13, 44, p. 1408.
5 DI I, II, 8, p. 7.
6 Cf. EDWARD F. CRANZ. "Development in Cusanus?" in: *Nicholas of Cusa and the Renaissance*, eds. Th. M. Izbicki, G. Christianson, Ashgate, Variorum, 2003, pp. 5–6; DI I, II, 5, p. 6.
7 Cf. DI I, II, 7, p. 7; II, III, 10, p. 10.
8 Cf. JEAN-MICHEL COUNET. "Introduction," in: Nicolas de Cues, *Les Conjectures,* Les Belles Lettres, Paris, 2011, pp. LXVII–LXVIII.
9 Cf. DI I, IV, 12, pp. 9–10.
10 Cf. AGNIESZKA KIJEWSKA. *"Idiota de mente": Cusanus' Position in the Debate between Aristotelianism and Platonism*, in: *Nicholas of Cusa on the Self and Self-Consciousness,* ed. W. A. Euler, Y. Gustafsson, I. Wikström, Abo Akademi University Press, Abo, 2010, pp. 67–88.
11 DI III, XI, 246, p. 141. Cf. CRANZ. "Development in Cusanus," pp. 6–7.
12 Cf. Ap 29–30, p. 480.
13 DB 37, p. 809.
14 Cf. VD IX, 39, p. 697; cf. CRANZ. "Reason and Beyond Reason," in: *Nicholas of Cusa and the Renaissance*, eds. Th. M. Izbicki, G. Christianson, Ashgate, Variorum, 2003, p. 25.
15 DB 5, p. 793.
16 VS 1, prol., p. 1280.
17 AT 8, p. 1426.

18 Cf. BARBARA GRONDKOWSKA. *Znaki i symbole. Filozofia w kazaniach Mikołaja z Kuzy* [*Signs and Symbols. Philosophy in Cusanus' Sermons*], Towarzystwo Naukowe KUL Press, Lublin, 2018, pp. 34–38; LAWRENCE F. HUNDERSMARCK. "Preaching," in: *Introducing Nicholas of Cusa. A Guide to a Renaissance Man*, eds. Ch. M. Bellitto, Th. M. Izbicki, G. Christianson, Paulist Press, New York-Mahwah, NJ, 2004, pp. 232–269.

19 Cf. TAMARA ALBERTINI. "Mathematics and Astronomy," in: *Introducing Nicholas of Cusa. A Guide to a Renaissance Man*, eds. Ch. M. Bellitto, Th. M. Izbicki, G. Christianson, Paulist Press, New York-Mahwah, NJ, 2004, pp. 373–375.

20 JEAN-MARIE NICOLLE. "Introduction," in: Nicolas de Cues, *Les écrits mathématiques*, ed. J.-M. Nicolle, Honoré Champion, Paris, 2007, p. 46.

21 Cf. WALTER A. EULER. "L'image de l'islam à la fin du Moyen Age. La correspondance entre Jean de Ségovie et Nicolas de Cues," in: *Nicolas de Cues et l'islam*, ed. H. Pasqua, Peeters, Louvain-la-Neuve, Louvain-Paris, 2013, pp. 9–20.

22 PF VI, 16, p. 640.

23 MICHEL DE CERTEAU. "The Gaze. Nicholas of Cusa," trans. by C. Porter, *Diacritics*, 17, 1987, p. 3.

24 Cf. JAMES E. BIECHLER. "Interreligious Dialogue," in: *Introducing Nicholas of Cusa. A Guide to a Renaissance Man*, eds. Ch. M. Bellitto, Th. M. Izbicki, G. Christianson, Paulist Press, New York-Mahwah, NJ, 2004, p. 283.

25 Cf. There, 284–285; cf. HERVE PASQUA. "Le Coran et le Fils de Dieu dans la 'Cribratio Alkorani'," in: *Nicolas de Cues et l'islam*. ed. H. Pasqua, Peeters, Louvain-la-Neuve, Louvain-Paris, 2013, pp. 159–174.

26 Cf. TOM KERGER. "La 'Cribratio Alkorani': un projet de dialogue avec l'islam," in: *Nicolas de Cues et l'islam*. ed. H. Pasqua, Peeters, Louvain-la-Neuve, Louvain-Paris, 2013, pp. 22–23.

4 The circle of Cusanus's reformatory activity

Before we begin the discussion of Cusanus's efforts to bring about reformation of both the ecclesiastical structures he was involved with and the moral conduct of his fellow Christians, it will be worthwhile to consider one significant fact. As Gerald Strauss observed, such Latin terms as *reformatio* and *renovatio* contain the prefix "re," whose original meaning in Latin carries the idea of a return to the original and presumably perfect state of things. This presupposes a point of view according to which no improvement can be effected in the course of time, but, on the contrary, the passage of time brings about ineluctable deterioration. Strauss has pointed to some scriptural sources of this assumption, among others he quotes St. Paul's Letter to the Romans 12, 2: *Do not be conformed to this world, but be transformed by the renewal of your mind*. Undoubtedly implied in this quote is a very negative evaluation of "this world," to which one ought not to conform. However, in the second clause of the quoted verse, St. Paul does not seem to imply any return to some past perfection when he urges his readers to "be transformed."[1]

This call for transformation and metamorphosis appears much better to correspond to the idea that inspired and directed Cusanus's spirited reformatory activity than any yearning for the lost perfection of the beginning. What he always strove to achieve in his efforts to improve the functioning of ecclesiastical and social structures and renew the spirituality of human beings involved therein was not so much a return to some original state but a spiritual transformation, a spiritual birth in fact, which aimed at ever fuller assimilation of an individual to Christ or/and to ever more perfect realization of sonship of God in a human person. Klaus Reinhardt found out that to begin with Nicholas developed his teaching on the inner transformation of a human being in a scheme of triple birth: the primeval birth of the Word within the Holy Trinity, the Incarnation of the Word and His birth in flesh and the third birth, which is again a birth of the Word, this time in the hearts of those who through their faith were made sons of God.[2]

DOI: 10.4324/9781003310693-4

This progression of the triple birth of the Word of God aims at leading human beings to the sonship of God, and such, in its essence, is the meaning of Cusanus's concept of *oiconomia*, which he found in and adopted from the Scriptures and the Fathers. As Dotan Leshem has shown in his study, in the Christian antiquity, three main senses of the word *oikonomia* were current. Two of them correspond exactly to the first two acts of birth mentioned by Cusanus. The first birth (the Word being born by the Father) corresponds to the third meaning of the word *oikonomia*, identified by Leshem:

> The third meaning, which was introduced by Tatian in the second century, describes the mode by which God the Father begets His Son, that is, the relationship between the Father and the son in the Godhead which will later occupy the centre of the debate between the orthodox and the Arians from the fourth century onward.[3]

The second birth of the Word, the one concerning Incarnation and the Word being born in flesh, is the correlate of the primary meaning of the term *oikonomia* in the patristic tradition. According to Leshem, this meaning of *oikonomia* was grounded on the reading of the Pauline Letters and taken up in the teaching of such writers as Clement of Alexandria and Origen, who incorporated it in the Platonic philosophical scheme. The movement set off by the Incarnation concerns both humanity as a whole and every human individual:

> On top of focusing on the centrality of the incarnation as the hermeneutical key, rendering *oikonomia* and incarnation synonymous many times, they combined personal and ecumenical enlightenment to go hand in hand leading each member and humanity as a whole to recapitulation at the fullness of ages. They combined macro-level, historical movement and micro-level of training and education of the individual. At the heart of both lies the economy of incarnation. In it, the Logos (i.e. God's Son) appears as pedagogue of the whole of humanity.[4]

Crucial for Cusanus's reformatory activity as the end and fulfilment thereof is the third birth, the birth of the Word in the human soul, which is conditioned by and grounded upon the first two births. "The birth of the Son in the soul" requires "the transformation of the mind," a reformation of the way of thinking which can only be effected by the agency of divine grace. One of the descriptions of the third birth is found in *Sermon* II, delivered by Nicholas for the feast of Epiphany of 1431:

> And [the intellect] follows this light of grace in order to apprehend where in that light Christ was born. Then comes the invisible sending of the Father's Splendor, viz., The Word of God in God. The sending is the

Begotten Wisdom's entering into the mind of the rational creature for the spiritual and free illumining of it. And although the Word of God – indeed, The Trinity as a whole – is everywhere, with respect to essence, nevertheless the Trinity is not everywhere with respect to its freely-given light. Accordingly, when in your darkened heathen-mind, or your less illuminated mind, a greater light arises and is begotten, then through the light of grace and by faith [in]formed by love you apprehend Christ born in you. Although this [birth] is the work of the Trinity, nevertheless the Son is born in you, because of the Brightness of eternal light.[5]

The economy of the reformatory efforts of Nicholas of Cusa was focused on the realization of the third birth of the Word, and this fact bears the responsibility for both successes and failures of his reforms. This can be seen throughout the history of his activity, starting from his participation in the debates of the Council of Basel and his first large-scale work, often described as a manifesto of conciliarism, *The Catholic Concordance*, in which many saw "the agenda for the Council of Basel for which all Europe was waiting impatiently."[6]

The conciliar movement of the 14th and 15th centuries was a very complex phenomenon and variously described and classified by historians. As Jovino de Guzman Miroy observed, the only points of agreement among the students of conciliarism are that it was a response to the crisis of the Great Schism in the Western Church, that its goal was a restoration of the unity of the Church under canonically elected and universally recognized pope and also that the apogee of conciliar movement was the Council of Constance held from 1414 to 1418, where the decree *Frequens* was issued, ruling that councils should be convoked every 5 years, which, however, was never put into practice. The following council of the Western Church, held in Basel starting from 1431, marked the beginning of the rapid decline of the movement.[7]

Conciliarism questioned the idea of the absolute supremacy of the pope (*plenitudo potestatis*) in the Church in both matters spiritual and political and instead attributed the plenitude of all ecclesiastical powers, including the judiciary and executive powers, to the legitimately convoked council representing the whole church; in the conciliarist view, such a council would also enjoy the privilege of infallibility.[8] Cusanus, who had studied documents issued by the past councils, including the ancient documents concerning the early ecumenical councils, was at first profoundly impressed by the power and efficiency of council decrees for the preservation of the public order and the maintenance of the orthodox faith.[9] In his *Concordance*, he undertook to study the three orders comprising the universal Church:

In my treatise on the Catholic concordance, I believe that it is necessary to examine that union of faithful people that is called the Catholic

Church, as well as the parts that together make up that church –
i.e., its soul and body. Therefore we will consider first the church
itself as a composite whole, then its soul, the holy priesthood, and
thirdly its body, the holy empire. And everything will be studied on
the basis of ancient approved sources, as necessary to understand the
substance, the nature, and the combinations and joinings of its members, so that we can know the sweet harmonious concordance that
produces eternal salvation and the safety of the commonwealth.[10]

Crucial for his work and for his whole concern with matters ecclesiastical is the idea of agreement (*concordantia*) between different orders
within the Church as a whole. The agreement between all the essential
constituents of the Church was the principle of the harmonious coexist-
ence and efficient cooperation of all the parts, the ecclesiastical whole,
and thus of the well-being of the Church. In the name of this universal
agreement, he distanced himself from all kinds of absolutism regarding
the constituent members of the Church, be it papal or conciliar absolutism. Initially a moderate conciliarist, he soon grew disappointed with
the Council of Basel and its ability to maintain the peace and agreement
within the ecclesiastical community and finally sided with Pope Eugene IV
against the rump conciliarist council. Therein were deep metaphysical reasons for that decision, as de Guzman Miroy has perspicaciously observed:

> Nevertheless, Cusanus' moderate conciliarism founded on a meta-
> physics of concordance was a true critique of absolutism, which does
> not lead to relativism or simple communitarianism. Even in the DCC,
> Cusanus was already championing the individual. As a critique of ab-
> solutism, the metaphysics of concordance provides a better solution
> than Basel's community sovereignty. The community might obscure
> the individual by demanding conformity and uniformity.[11]

According to Cusanus, the complete and absolute power is the at-
tribute of God alone; the hierarchically structured created reality is a
development of that power, extending from universal cosmic realities
down to single individuals. The structure of the Church should exactly
mirror the order of this outpouring of the Infinite Divine Light and by
this assimilation should lead humanity to the unity with that Light.[12]
The ultimate goal of the whole movement of reality is assimilation to
Christ, that is the third birth of the Word in human reality. This birth
concerns human individuals as well as the Church as a whole:

> In summary therefore, we may say that Christ is the way, the truth,
> and the life, and the head of all creatures, the husband or spouse
> of the church, which is constituted in a concordance of all rational

creatures – with him as the One, and among themselves, the many – in various [hierarchical] gradations.[13]

Every human being may have his assigned place in the hierarchical reality of humanity reborn and transformed in the form of the Church, whose foundation is the transcendent spiritual Principle.[14] The salvific plan – *oikonomia* – of that Principle, the Word, extends to all human individuals, each taken in his/her unique character. From this general theoretical insight, some determinate consequences follow: (1) the point of reference and absolute standard of evaluation for all values being realized in the created world (social, political, economic and moral values) is found within the transcendent Principle, which manifests Itself in the human world while always remaining pure in Its transcendence and inaccessible to any material agency; (2) every structure within the created reality is a projection and development of the superior power of its transcendent Source; this surpassing power cannot be arrogated or claimed by any constituent element of that created structure; (3) an indispensable condition for created structures properly to fulfil their assigned functions is agreement and harmonious collaboration (*concordia*) between their constituent elements; and (4) the ground for this agreement and collaboration is the acceptance of one ultimate goal for all, which is assimilation to Christ or, to say the same thing in another way, a fulfilment of the divine *oikonomia* with regard to an individual human being and humanity as a whole.

Having adopted an attitude based on such assumptions, Cusanus did not find it easy to conduct his ecclesiastical and political activity, whether at the council of Basel or elsewhere. In May 1437, in the company of two other disillusioned council fathers, he finally left Basel and henceforth devoted his energies to the task of reforming the Church as a papal envoy: the "Hercules of Eugenians." Cusanus's missions, the one that bore fruit in the shape of the Concordat of Vienna in 1448 and the one devoted to dispensing the indulgences of the Jubilee of 1450, earned him as many adherents and supporters as implacable opponents. During his reformatory activity, Cusanus convoked 12 local synods, issued 13 decrees and visited about 80 religious institutions. The program of the reform of diocesan clergy he attempted to carry out focused on resolute prohibition of concubinage of priests and ecclesiastical simony and on precise injunctions concerning the celebration of the Eucharist and Eucharistic processions. These injunctions had to do with some widespread devotional practices of the time, which occasionally verged on superstition and excessive familiarity with the holy. This feature of the popular religion of the time was commented upon by Johan Huizinga:

This fatuous familiarity with God in daily life has to be seen in two ways. On the one hand, it testifies to the absolute stability and immediacy of faith, but where this familiarity becomes habitual it increases the danger that the godless (who are always with us), but also the pious, in moments of insufficient religious tension, will continuously profane faith more or less consciously and intentionally. In particular, the most tender of mysteries, the Eucharist, is threatened in this way. (...) Life was permeated by religion to the degree that the distance between the earthly and the spiritual was in danger of being obliterated at any moment. While on the one hand all of ordinary life was raised to the sphere of the divine, on the other the divine was bound to the mundane in an indissoluble mixture with daily life.[15]

Cusanus's concern about the properly respectful attitude of the simple believers to the Eucharist, went hand-in-hand with a firm opposition to what he considered to be superstitious practices, and in particular to the widespread cult of bleeding hosts.[16] Very much concerned about inculcating the believers with the enlightened Christian consciousness, he called for Christians to turn their backs on the spurious miracles and embrace instead the simple and sure devotion to sacraments. Some of his decisions caused much grievance among the faithful and were appealed against to the pope himself; nevertheless, the sincerity of his efforts to instill the principles of pure and uncontaminated Christian belief into the minds of his faithful is beyond question. He was keenly aware of the danger of unwittingly replacing the worship of true God with an idolatrous cult of mere creatures. Such acts of turning away from true God to creatures he calls idolatry or adultery, which are opposed to true faithfulness:

By the word "faithfulness" [on the part of the soul] we ought to understand that the soul not be adulterous and not seek out lovers other than its Bridegroom. Now, the soul seeks out other lovers when it directs itself, by choice, to creatures; and the more it clings to creatures, the less it clings to God. But this attachment to creatures can be of two kinds: On the one hand, [the attachment occurs] because [the soul] seeks something divine in the creation, and it embraces as divine *that something* in the creation; and [this embracing] is idolatry. On the other hand, [the soul] seeks in the creation some remedy as coming from the creation.[17]

Even this cursory overview makes it evident that at the heart of Nicholas's reformatory activity was a concern for uncompromising purity, as Scott Hendrix put it. However, what Cusanus sought in his efforts was not a return to the purity modelled, for instance, on the first Christian communities as described in the Acts, what he meant was a realization of the ideal contained in early church canons confirming the post-apostolic tradition.[18] According to Donald Sullivan, Cusanus's reforming strategy can be clearly seen in his activity: he strove at sincere edification of the faithful and at reforming the liturgy and religious practices in general according to the principles of the canon law, the synodal decrees and the spirit of rigorous asceticism espoused by the movement of *devotio moderna*.[19]

The reform of monastic life put forward by himself in principle reduced to the demand for the monks to observe their monastic rule in its original purity and avoided exposing themselves to the influences of the secular life and relaxation of the monastic discipline. In 1451, he even set up a commission, consisting of some Cistercian, Benedictine and Augustinian monks, to work out the scheme of the implementation of the postulated reforms. As bishop of Brixen, he tried to carry out his reform in the monasteries of his diocese, which, however, resulted in a long-lasting clash with the prioress of the Benedictine abbey of Sonnenburg, Verena von Stuben.[20]

Nevertheless not all monasteries resisted his efforts to implement a reform. The Benedictine community of the abbey of St. Quirin in Tegernsee offered him much goodwill and support, the fact testified to by the exchange of letters between Nicholas and the abbots of St. Quirin: Kaspar Aindorffer and Bernhard von Waging. To these two abbots, Nicholas dedicated his very original work *On the Vision of God*.[21] Many years after Johannes Trithemius, abbot of the Benedictine abbey of Sponheim wrote the following eulogy on the subject of Cusanus's mission in Germany and its effects:

> Nicholas of Cusa appeared in Germany as an angel of light and peace, amidst darkness and confusion, restored the unity of the Church, strengthened the authority of her Supreme Head, and sowed a precious seed of new life.[22]

Notes

1 Cf. GERALD STRAUSS. "Ideas of 'Reformatio' and 'Renovatio' from the Middle Ages to the Reformation," in: *Handbook of European History, 1400-1600: Late Middle Ages, Renaissance, and Reformation*, vol. II: *Visions, Programs and Outcomes*, eds. Th. A. Brady. H. A. Oberman, J. D. Tracy, Brill, Leiden, 1995, pp. 11–12.

2 Cf. KLAUS REINHARDT. "L'idée de naissance de Dieu dans l'ame chez Nicolas de Cues et l'influence d'Eckhart," in: *La naissance de Dieu dans l'âme chez Eckhart et Nicolas de Cues*, ed. M.-A. Vannier, Cerf, Paris, 2006, pp. 88–89.

3 DOTAN LESHEM. "Oikonomia," *in: The Routledge Handbook of Economic Theology*, ed. S. Schwarzkopf, Routledge, London-New York, 2020, p. 274; Cf. GIORGIO AGAMBEN. *The Kingdom and the Glory*, trans. by L. Chiesa, M. Mandarni, Stanford University Press, Stanford, CA, 2011, p. 35.

4 LESHEM. "Oikonomia," p. 275; cf. AGAMBEN. *The Kingdom and the Glory*, p. 37.

5 S-1 II, III, 25, p. 36.

6 STRAUSS. "Ideas of 'Reformatio'," p. 11.

7 Cf. JOVINO DE GUZMAN MIROY. *Tracing Nicholas of Cusa's Early Development*, The Relationship between "De concordantial catholica "and "De docta ignorantia. " Peeters, Leuven, Louvain-la-Neuve, 2009, pp. 46–49.

48   *The circle of Cusanus's reformatory activity*

8   There, pp. 67–68; cf. AGAMBEN. *The Kingdom and the Glory*, pp. 100–104.
9   Cf. CC I, praef. 2, p. 3.
10 CC I, praef. 3, p. 4.
11 MIROY. *Tracing Nicholas of Cusa's Early Development*, p. 75. Cf. JOACHIM STIEBER. "The Hercules of the Eugenians' at the Crossroads: Nicholas of Cusa's Decision for the Pope Against the Council in 1436-37 – Theological, Political, and Social Aspect," in: *Nicholas of Cusa. In Search of God and Wisdom*, ed. G. Christianson, Th. Izbicki, Brill, Leiden, 1991, p. 242.
12 Cf. CC I, VII, 41, pp. 27–28; cf. DONALD SULLIVAN. "Cusanus and Pastoral Renewal: The Reform of Popular Religion in the Germanies," in: *Nicholas of Cusa on Christ and the Church*, eds. G. Christianson, Th. M. Izbicki, Leiden-New York-Köln, 1996, pp. 166–167.
13 CC I, I, 8, p. 7.
14 Cusanus's position is contrary to the "Capitalist theology of providence," as M. Dempsey says: "Scholars have long observed the way economics functions as an ersatz religion (…) in which the market itself *is* God (…). Here we may add that if God is posited as the condition for the possibility of market order, then God *cannot* be more than an immanent ground of nature. By itself, natural theology offers no knowledge of God beyond the world. (…) Thus, the capitalist notion of 'God' as the invisible hand is simply extrapolated from efficiency, order, and equilibrium to explain market order, while legitimizing an economic system with natural theology." (Cf. MICHAEL T. DEMPSEY. "Providence," in: *The Routledge Handbook of Economic Theology*, ed. S. Schwarzkopf, Routledge, London-New York, 2020, p. 23.)
15 JOHAN HUIZINGA. *The Autumn of the Middle Ages*, trans. by R. J. Payton, U. Mammitzsch, The University of Chicago Press, Chicago, 1996, pp. 178–179.
16 Cf. MORIMISCHI WATANABE. *Nicholas of Cusa – A Companion to His Life and His Times,* ed. G. Christianson, Th. M. Izbicki, Burlington, 2011, pp. 30–31.
17 S-1 XXI, 13, p. 350.
18 Cf. SCOTT H. HENDRIX. "Nicholas of Cusa's Ecclesiology Between Reform and Reformation," in: *Nicholas of Cusa on Christ and the Church*, eds. G. Christianson, Th. M. Izbicki, Leiden-New York-Köln, 1996, p. 119.
19 Cf. SULLIVAN, "Cusanus and Pastoral Renewal," pp. 172–173.
20 Cf. WATANABE. *Nicholas of Cusa – A Companion*, pp. 204–207.
21 Cf. There, pp. 210–213.
22 Quotation after: WATANABE. *Nicholas of Cusa – A Companion*, p. 31.

5 The circles of the game

To illustrate the way Cusanus represented the third birth of the Word, the Son of God being born in the soul of a believer and how this crucial event of the human life, transforming man into another son of God, should take place, let me take a closer look at the content of one of the last works he wrote, the dialogue *The Bowling-Game*, occasionally also referring to other texts that came from his pen. Cusanus's students date the composition of that work to 1463, when the Cardinal of St. Peter in Chains stayed at Rome, although there is some disagreement as to the precise moment: while Vansteenberghe believes both books of the dialogue to have been written in October of that year,[1] the editor of that work, Hans G. Senger, quoting the findings of Erich Meuthen, supposes the first book to have been written before 6 March 1463 and the second after that date. The idea of writing this work may have occurred to the author in the summer of 1462, when he took a period of rest at Orvieto.[2] Both books of the dialogue conclude with compositions in verse whose author was not Nicholas himself, although they are found in the two manuscripts which formed the basis for the critical edition of the dialogue: the codex 219 of the Library of St. Nicholas Hospital in Kues and the manuscript of Cracow Jagiellonian Library, signature 682.[3] It is not unlikely that Cusanus himself saw to it that these pieces of verse be included in the handwritten copies of his work, which would suggest that their author belonged to the circle of his close associates. The likely suggestions as to the authorship include Andrea de Bussi, Cusanus's secretary and amanuensis and even Pope Pius II, whose passion for composing verse was widely known.[4] *The Bowling-Game* is written in the form of dialogue between the Cardinal of St. Peter in Chains and, at first, Prince John, son of Otto I Count Palatine of Mosbach of the House of Wittelsbach, and then Albert IV, Prince of Bavaria and a relative of John.[5] Both of Cusanus's interlocutors are members of a ruling family with royal and even imperial connections; both are hopeful young men claiming to be inexperienced and therefore desirous of instruction. The cardinal, in a true Socratic fashion, undertakes to conduct them through

DOI: 10.4324/9781003310693-5

twists and turns of intellectual debate, beginning with simple and obvious things of everyday experience and then proceeding step by step toward consideration of profound and serious matters normally hidden under the surface of everyday phenomena. A good starting point for the philosophical conversation in *The Bowling Game* was provided by the consideration of the popular game of bowling, then a novel and fashionable form of amusement:

> *John:* All of us are fascinated with this new and fun game – perhaps because in it there is a symbolism of a certain deep speculation, a symbolism that we ask to have explained. *Cardinal:* You are rightly moved [to ask]. For certain sciences have instruments and games: arithmetic has the rhithmatia; music has the monochord; and even the game of chess is not devoid of the symbolism of moral [lessons]. I believe that no decent game is altogether lacking in [symbolic] learning. For example, this very fun game of bowling, it seems to me, symbolizes for us no small amount of philosophy.[6]

The Cardinal, the leader and preceptor in this dialogue, makes the observation that both the ball to be rolled in the game of bowls and the game itself are creations of human intelligence, for no other living thing on earth is capable of inventing games, even though some animals may occasionally behave in a playful way:

> For no beast makes a bowling-ball and makes it move toward a goal. Therefore, you see that these works of man are done by means of a power that surpasses [the powers of] other animals of this world.[7]

Thus it can be concluded that for Cusanus, playing a game is a specifically human action with a sense and meaning of its own, and a game itself, with its fixed rules and conventional purposefulness and meaning, belongs to the domain of specifically human creations, as it bears the imprint of the faculty of understanding and comprehension. And yet animals can play too: Johan Huizinga, having observed that animals "play just like men," saw in play and playing a prefiguration and one of the sources of culture as such:

> Here we have at once a very important point: even in its simplest forms on the animal level, play is more than a mere physiological phenomenon or a psychological reflex. It goes beyond the confines of purely physical or purely biological activity. It is a *significant* function – that is to say, there is some sense to it. In play there is something 'at play' which transcends the immediate needs of life and imparts meaning to the action. All play means something. If we call

the active principle that makes up the essence of play, 'instinct', we explain nothing; if we call it 'mind' or 'will' we say too much. However we may regard it, the very fact that play has a meaning implies a non-materialistic quality in the nature of the thing itself.[8]

At this point, it may be worthwhile to stop and consider some features of a game/play which can help us to see why it provided a convenient starting point for a parenetic Socratic dialogue under the lead of Cusanus.

As Huizinga aptly observed, (1) play is "more than a mere physiological phenomenon"; it "goes beyond" the ordinary, biologically determined process of life, characterized by the necessity to satisfy the natural needs and irresistible drives; from the point of view of mere biological subsistence, play is entirely superfluous. Play belongs to the domain of free, voluntary activity, which formed the content of the part of life that the ancients called *otium* (leisure). This total unconcern with the ordinary and necessary business of living is what playing has in common with all spiritual activities: art, literature, religion, and also various kinds of amusement. In particular, participating in games has common features with that spiritual exercise, which Hadot and later Foucault took to form the essence of philosophizing.[9] Independent of, and, so to say, set above the practical concerns of existence, playing at a game is nevertheless capable (2) of completely engrossing the player, of occupying his whole attention and of drawing him into the game's own artificial space, the fictional world, regulated by (3) the conventionally established principles and laws of its own. Huizinga remarks:

> Summing up the formal characteristics of play we may call it a free activity standing quite consciously outside 'ordinary' life as being 'not serious', but at the same time absorbing the player intensely and utterly. It is an activity connected with no material interest, and no profit can be gained by it. It proceeds within its own proper boundaries of time and space according to fixed rules and in an orderly manner.[10]

Cusanus in the dialogue points out to his young friend "the boundaries of time and space" and the "fixed rules" of the game of bowls that attracted the young man's attention:

> And I made a mark where we stand throwing the bowling-ball; and in the middle of the level-surface I made a circle, at whose center there is the throne of a king, whose kingdom is a kingdom-of-life enclosed within the circle; and within the [one large] circle I made nine other circles. Now, the game's directions require that the bowling-ball came to rest within a circle and that a ball closer to the center scores more

points – according to the number assigned to the circle where the ball stops. And he who most quickly scores thirty-four points – which correspond to the number of Christ's life – is the winner.[11]

Artificial as it is, this fixed world of the game remains nevertheless in a certain definite relation to reality, and it is a reduced imitation of it; thus, grasping the principles and order of the game can open the way to comprehension of the actual world, and conversely, comprehension of the world can enhance the efficiency of one's performance in the game. This is the meaning of the Cardinal's observation:

> These and many other factors must, it seems to me, be subtly noted, on account of the similarity of art and nature. For since art imitates nature, we attain [a knowledge of] the powers of nature by means of the things that we subtly discover in art.[12]

Clearly, the Cardinal regards a game as a key and invitation to consideration of the Universe and its inner structure and working. This assumption emphasizes one more essential feature of playing a game: (4) "It is a *significant* function – that is to say, there is some sense to it." However, if the game we are playing is a significant, symbolic structure, those who play that game must be able to read and interpret the meaning of that structure and its component parts, and in other words, they must be rational players.[13] It follows that (5) those who engage in playing a game consisting of fixed rules regulating a coherent set of actions (as opposed to mere playful behavior of animals) must be creatures capable of rational comprehension and conscious application of the principles of the game; in short, they must have intelligence at the level of human beings. True, Ken Binmore is right to observe:

> But game theory isn't able to solve all of the world's problems, because it only works when people play games *rationally*. So it can't predict the behaviour of love-sick teenagers like Romeo or Juliet, or madman like Hitler or Stalin. However, people don't always behave irrationally, and so it isn't waste of time to study what happens when people put on their thinking caps.[14]

The Cardinal in the dialogue, a mature and wise man, eminent dignitary of the Church, faces the challenging task of engaging in a didactic dialogue with young men, who will soon shoulder the task of the exercise of political power, with the purpose of forming them into rational, responsible and prudent "players," participants in the supreme game of political life, who will be able to comprehend the sense of the game and teach and introduce others into constructive and meaningful participation in it. The highest competence in the game of politics, as well as in other games, calls for (6) the knowledge of one's own self and the ability rationally to evaluate one's own powers and weaknesses. The sober and realistic appreciation of one's dispositions and skills will enable one better to perfect one's abilities and seek new accomplishments, which will enhance one's chances of success.[15]

Any game involves an element of competition, (7) rivalry, even outright fight, which is the source not only of uncertainty as to the final result but also of the interest and fascination. However, the most important kind of fight involved in a game appears to be the struggle against one's own weaknesses: laziness, indecision, cowardice and ignorance. In order to achieve mastery of the game, it is necessary to overcome one's limitations, enrich one's vision and broaden one's room for action. A committed player will always strive to develop his competence in the game and increase his efficiency in order to maximize his own power and minimize the influence of what we call chance (8) upon the final result. Prince John notices the interplay of the action directed by intention and chance in the development of the game:

> However, since the ball does not always come to a stop at the center of the circle, where each player intends to place it, and since one of the players [succeeds in] placing the ball at one time near the center, but at a subsequent time (although he has the same intention as before) the ball veers far from the center, we speak of its seeming to be the case that the ball is moved not only in accordance with the intention of the thrower but also in accordance with chance.[16]

The chance, which cannot be totally excluded from the game, is the source of the element of risk (9) always involved in playing games, the risk that our efforts to achieve the goal of the game may be frustrated by a chance factor beyond our control. (10) The purpose of the game is to achieve a state of fulfilment and rest in which nothing more is desired as far as the game is concerned and nothing more needs to be performed, a state analogous to complete happiness. The Cardinal represents this successful finish of the game as symbolic of the ultimate fulfilment of human life, the coming into the Kingdom of Life:

> This game, I say, symbolizes the movement of our soul from its own kingdom unto the Kingdom of Life, in which there is eternal rest and eternal happiness. In the Center of the Kingdom of Life our King and Life-Give, Christ Jesus, presides. When He was like unto us, He moved the bowling-ball of His own person in such a way that it would come to rest at the Center of Life. He left us an example in order that we would do just as He had done and in order that our

bowling-ball would follow [in the pathway of] His, although it is impossible that another ball come to rest at the [exact] same Center of Life at which Christ's ball comes to rest. For within a circle there are an infinite number of places and mansions.[17]

In order to achieve success in the game, one should receive appropriate training, preferably under the supervision of an expert (11), that is a person who, having achieved mastery in the skill necessary to perform the game, has proved his expertise by his own excellent performance. Thus far, the discussed essential features of the organized social competitive activity practiced merely as a form of amusement, which is essentially that which we call a game, pointed to the analogy existing between this playful occupation and the serious business of living: any game in its fixed order of actions, in its structured setting, in its artificial purposefulness, is a simplified symbolic representation of the real activity of living and its striving to achieve the ultimate purpose of life.

There is, however, another interesting analogy that can be drawn concerning playing games, namely the analogy between a game and (12) a liturgical representation of holy mysteries. The sacred performance of a liturgy, although lacking the competitive element, can also be looked upon as a sort of play, as a very special kind of theater. There is indeed a very special claim made concerning liturgy that sets it apart from other theatricals, namely that a liturgical performance makes real and present here and now that which it represents. This is how Huizinga described a liturgical representation:

> The sacred performance is more than an actualization in appearance only, a sham reality; it is also more than a symbolical actualization – it is a mystical one. In it, something invisible and inactual takes beautiful, actual, holy form. The participants in the rite are convinced that the action actualizes and effects a definite beatification, brings about an order of things higher than that in which they customarily live. All the same this "actualization by representation" still retains the formal characteristics of play in every respect. It is played or performed within a playground that is literally "staked out," and played moreover as a feast, i.e. in mirth and freedom. A sacred space, a temporarily real world of its own, has been expressly hedged off for it. But with the end of the play its effect is not lost; rather it continues to shed its radiance on the ordinary world outside, a wholesome influence working security, order and prosperity for the whole community until the sacred play-season comes round again.[18]

Seen in this perspective, the category of play becomes a symbolic representation extending to all aspects of real life, including the most elevated and holy: both a competitive game and a sacred performance of a liturgical act can be looked upon as enacted representations of the supreme and all-comprehensive mystery of human life. In this way, they become suitable vehicles for serious consideration of the most essential matters concerning human existence. Now we can see and appreciate the deep reasons why Nicholas of Cusa has chosen discussion of a game as a suitable means to convey his philosophical and Christian message. If a game can be looked upon as representing the *universum* of human life, it can also be shown to represent the ultimate mysteries of the drama of life, which is the birth of the Word, that is, Christ in the soul of a human being, and the journey of the human soul toward its center and source, that is toward God.[19] In Cusanus 's approach, a game not only assumes the function of a liturgical act, which shows a certain reality, but also makes it present here and now in a way; the language of the game becomes in a way performative language. Cusanus's symbol-oriented approach can be seen as characteristic of Christianity in general. Giorgio Agamben, referring to some texts by Odo Casel OSB, one of the moving spirits of the renewal of liturgy in the Catholic Church at the beginning of the 20th century, believed liturgy to be essential to Christianity:

> Christianity (…) it is rather a "mystery," that is, a liturgical *action*, a "performance," whose actors are Christ and his mystical body, namely, the Church. And this action is, of course, a specific praxis, but at the same time, it defines the most universal and truest human activity, in which what is at stake is the salvation of those who carry it out and of those who participate in it. Liturgy ceases, from this perspective, to appear as the celebration of an exterior rite, which has its truth elsewhere (in faith and in dogma): on the contrary, only in the carrying out *hic et nunc* of this absolutely performative action, which always realizes what it signifies, can believers find their truth and their salvation. According to Casel, in fact, liturgy (…) is not a "representation" or a "commemoration" of the salvific event: it is itself the event.[20]

Thus in the light of the discussion carried out in *The Bowling Game* and its underlying assumptions, our life and its activity appear to be participation in a universal, archetypal game, the game of games, the game, which is the drama of existence itself. All of us are called upon to accept the conditions of the participation in this game, comply with its rules and perform the prescribed actions necessary to achieve the purpose thereof. If we willingly accept this call, we enter into the order of the divine *oiko-nomia*, God's plan of universal salvation which is being carried out in the process of history. This historical economy follows the pattern of the Trinitarian *oikonomia*, the eternal birth of the Son from the Father, in that the Son, the Divine Word, is again being born, this time in the souls of men who have willingly obeyed the call to enter the game. These men, in whose souls the Christ is again born, become adoptive sons of the Father by virtue of the grace they receive. The transformation caused in the souls of the faithful by the birth of the Word in them has been referred to in the Greek patristic tradition, and in the West above all by Scottus Eriugena, as *deificatio/theosis*.[21] Cusanus, an assiduous reader of both Pseudo-Dionysius and John Scotus, also adopted both the theme and the language of deification, as is made evident by the following quote:

> I judge that being a son of God is to be regarded as nothing other than deification, which, in Greek, is called *theosis*. But you know that *theosis* is ultimacy-of-perfection, which is called both knowledge of God and His Word and intuitive vision. For John the theologian's meaning is, I believe, that Logos, or Eternal Reason, which in the beginning was God-with-God, gave to man rational light when He gave to him a spirit in His own likeness. Thereafter, [God] declared (by means of various admonitions from the seer-prophets and, in the end, by means of the Word, which appeared in the world) that the light of reason is the life of our spirit and that (in the case of us believers) if we have accepted the Divine Word Himself, then there arises in our rational spirit the power of sonship.[22]

The deification of a human being, the transformation of him into an adoptive son of God, turns out to be the ultimate purpose of the arch-game of human life, which brings the perfect satisfaction of all desires and absolute fulfilment and happiness. Nothing less than deification can be the suitable end of this all-encompassing game which is human life. This final fulfilment can be also described as assimilation to Christ since the person of Christ appears both to be the final cause of the game and the only suitable means and method of the progress in the course thereof. Last but not least, a successful result of one's participation in the game enables one to render glory to God in the proper and fitting way, for only a person transformed into a Christ and a son of God will be able to value God's glory above his own life[23]:

> He is a Christian who prefers the glory of God to his own life and glory and who prefers it in such a way that if he were tested by persecution, he would be found to be just such [a convinced believer]. Christ lives in him, but he himself does not live. Therefore, he is a despiser of this world and of this life; in him, through faith, there is the spirit of the Son of God, Jesus Christ; and having died to the world, he is alive in Christ.[24]

Thus, we can conclude that the Cardinal in the dialogue succeeds in using the discussion of an organized social diversion which is playing a game with fixed rules as an introduction into a serious philosophical speculation on the most essential and the most sublime matters that are of concern to human beings. In this way, he followed in the footsteps of the philosophers of antiquity, who in simple phenomena of human everyday experience found a springboard catapulted them onto the heights where the contemplation and discussion of the matters of ultimate importance became open to them. In a novel and inspiring Christian context, Cusanus continues the philosophical approach of the ancients, who found in philosophy a form of spiritual exercise as described by Hadot. To use the categories of the last named, there appears to be a profound connection and unity between the learning to live, to enter into a dialogue with others, to die and to read. Both in his days and in other times, there could have been few men who equaled the cardinal of St. Peter in Chains in the mastery of these arts.[25]

Notes

1 Cf. EDMOND VANSTEENBERGHE. *Le cardinal Nicolas de Cues*, Honoré Champion, Paris, 1920 (repr. Minerva GMBH, Frankfurt am Main, 1963), p. 275.
2 Cf. HANS G. SENGER. "Praefatio editoris," in: Nicolai de Cusa, *De ludo globi, Opera omnia* vol. IX, ed. H. G. Senger, Felix Meiner Verlag, Hamburgi 1998, pp. XXIII–XXIV; HANS G. SENGER. "Jeu de la boule," in : *Encyclopédie des mystiques rhénans. D'Eckhart à Nicolas de Cues et leur réception.* ed. Maire-Anne Vannier, Cerf, Paris, 2011, p. 675.
3 The manuscript from Jagellonian Library from 1495 belonged to Michael Falkenberg (1460–1534), professor of Arts at Cracow University. Cf. W. SENKO, Z. WŁODEK. "Les manuscrits des oeuvres de Nicolas de Cues conservés en Pologne." *Mediaevalia Philosophica Polonorum*, 13, 1968, p. 95.
4 Cf. SENGER. "Praefatio editoris," pp. XXVIII–XXIX. Andrea de Bussi was a pioneer of printing in Italy and claimed that Cusanus had a great interest in the art of printing. Cf. DERMOT MORAN. "Nicholas of Cusa and Modern philosophy," in: *The Cambridge Companion to Renaissance Philosophy*, ed. by J. Hankins, Cambridge University Press, Cambridge, 2007, p. 190, endnote 13.
5 Cf. LG II, 61, p. 1211.
6 LG I, 1, p. 1182.
7 LG, I, 3, p. 1182.
8 JOHAN HUIZINGA. *Homo ludens. A Study of the Play-element in culture*, trans. by R. F. C. Hull, Routledge and Kegan Paul, London, 2002, p. 1.
9 Cf. PIERRE HADOT. *Philosophy as a Way of Life: Spiritual Exercises from Socrates to Foucault*, ed. by A. Davidson, trans. by M. Chase, Blackwell Publishers, 1995, Blackwell Publishers, Malden, MA, 1995 pp. 23–24, 81–82. About the relation of Michel Foucault to Pierre Hadot, see: MARTA FAUSTINO, GIANFRANCO FERRARO (eds.). *The Late Foucault. Ethical and Political Questions*, Bloomsbury Academic, London-New York-Oxford-New Delhi-Sydney, 2020.
10 HUIZINGA. *Homo ludens*, p. 13; f. KEN BINMORE. *Game Theory. A Very Short Introduction*, Oxford University Press, Oxford, 2007, pp. 57–58.

11 LG I, 50, p. 1207.
12 LG I, 7, p. 1184.
13 Cf. HUIZINGA. *Homo ludens*, pp. 105–106.
14 KEN BINMORE. *Game theory*, p. 2.
15 LG I, 3, p. 1182.
16 LG I, 55, p. 1210; I, 57, p. 1211.
17 LG I, 51, p. 1207.
18 HUIZINGA. *Homo ludens*, p. 14.
19 Cf. LAWRENCE H. BOND. "The Journey of the Soul to God in Nicholas of Cusa's 'De ludo globi'," in: *Nicholas of Cusa. In Search of God and Wisdom*, eds. G. Christianson, Th. Izbicki, Brill, Leiden, 1991, pp. 71–72.
20 GIORGIO AGAMBEN. *Creation and Anarchy. The Work of Art and the Religion of Capitalism,* trans. by A. Kotsko, Stanford University Press, Stanford, CA, 2019, p. 10.
21 Cf. ARISTOTLE PAPANIKOLAU. "Theosis," in: *The Oxford Handbook of Mystical Theology,* eds. E. Howells, M. A. McIntosh, Oxford University Press, Oxford, 2020, pp. 569–585; NANCY J. HUDSON. *Becoming God. The Doctrine of Theosis in Nicholas of Cusa*, The Catholic University of America Press, Washington, D.C., 2007, pp. 134–178.
22 DF 52, p. 341.
23 Cf. AGAMBEN. *The Kingdom and the Glory,* trans. by L. Chiesa, M. Mandarni, Stanford University Press, Stanford, CA, 2011, pp. 197–200.
24 LG I, 53, p. 1208.
25 Cf. HADOT. *Philosophy as a Way of Life*, pp. 81–144.

6 Two more circles in the game

The circles of The creator and of The creation

As was already observed in Chapter 5, playing at a game snatches man away for a moment from the world of his everyday routine and transports him into the surroundings of an invented cosmos of its own. However, it was also remarked that the cosmos of the game, artificial as it is, is not totally alien to the actual world of ours; on the contrary, it bears a definite relation to the reality of our experience; its structure is a simplified reflection of the order of the Universe and, as such, may be of help to us in our efforts to understand the way the Universe is built and works. It is precisely this kind of help, obtained from the consideration of the game under discussion, that the Cardinal in the dialogue uses to elucidate certain matters concerning metaphysics and cosmology.

The game of bowls as described in Nicholas's dialogue used some requisites: there was a ball, roundish, but not perfectly round in shape, slightly elongated and curved with different parts of it having different curvature so that, when thrown, it moved along a spiral path. The game was played on a flat surface with nine concentric circles marked on it.

The ball having been set in motion, the course of its movement depended on its lop-sided shape as well as on the direction and force given it by the thrower. The path followed by it, we are told by the Cardinal, was slightly different at every instance of a throw: just as there are no two absolutely identical balls, so there are no two cases of one ball moving exactly in the same way. This statement is as much a conclusion drawn from observation as a result of the application of the general principle emphasized by the nominalist school of thought: there are no two individual things or events that could be absolutely and in every respect identical:

> When someone throws a bowling-ball, he does not hold it in his hand at one time in the same way as at another time; or he does not release it in the same way or does not place it on the ground in the same way or does not impel it with an equal force. For it is not possible that anything be done twice in exactly the same way. For it involves a contradiction [to say] that there are two and that they are in every

DOI: 10.4324/9781003310693-6

respect equal, without any difference. For how could a plurality of things be a plurality apart from any difference?[1]

However, the shape of the ball and its peculiar movement are not themselves of much interest to the participants of the conversation; they are just a handy means of introducing a topic that will lead them, as if "by the hand" to discussion of a philosophically really important matter; in this case, the object of the discussion will be the shape and movement of the Universe. Cosmological speculation was very close to Cusanus's heart from the outset of his serious involvement with philosophy. Already in the work *On Learned Ignorance*, anticipating, according to some interpreters, the position of Copernicus and Galileo, he affirmed that the Universe lacks a natural or geometrical center and a circumference, nor is it divided into two spheres different between themselves as to their physical properties: the sublunary and the celestial sphere, which was a dogma of Aristotelian cosmology.[2] This much is affirmed by the Cardinal in the dialogue:

> Hence, if we consider the various movements of the spheres, [we will see that] it is not possible for the world-machine to have, as a fixed and immovable center, either our perceptible earth or air or fire or any other thing. For, with regard to motion, we do not come to an unqualifiedly minimum—i.e., to a fixed center. For the [unqualifiedly] minimum must coincide with the [unqualifiedly] maximum; therefore, the center of the world coincides with the circumference. Hence, the world does not have a [fixed] circumference. For if it had a [fixed] center, it would also have a [fixed] circumference; and hence it would have its own beginning and end within itself, and it would be bounded in relation to something else, and beyond the world there would be both something else and space (locus). But all these [consequences] are false. Therefore, since it is not possible for the world to be enclosed between a physical center and [a physical] circumference, the world—of which God is the center and the circumference—is not understood. And although the world is not infinite, it cannot be conceived as finite, because it lacks boundaries within which it is enclosed. Therefore, the earth, which cannot be the center, cannot be devoid of all motion.[3]

The theses advanced in this passage as to the structure of the world-machine must have appeared as startlingly novel to many of Nicholas's contemporaries: no fixed center of the Universe, the Earth is no more the center than any other point in outer space, no circumference, indeed, no spatial boundaries of cosmic space. Any limits of the Universe in space are unthinkable, for they presuppose something outside it, and nothing can be thought as existing outside the all-encompassing cosmos. All this will appear difficult to grasp, given the assumptions of traditional cosmology. Thus, the Cardinal concludes:

> Thereupon you will see—through the intellect, to which only learned ignorance is of help—that the world and its motion and shape cannot be apprehended. For [the world] will appear as a wheel in a wheel and a sphere in a sphere—having its center and circumference nowhere, as was stated.[4]

Invoked here is Cusanus's famous concept of learned unknowing[5]: this undoubtedly suggests that the participants of the dialogue are embarking upon consideration of matters that not only seem to be novel and difficult to grasp but also, indeed, lie at the extreme limits of comprehensibility. Such is the question of the roundness of the Universe, that can be "seen" by the intellect, although it is invisible in itself. The roundness of the world consists in a point which is a single and indivisible unit, an atom that cannot be multiplied. This point defines the height of a circle, all that lies at an equal distance from the center of it. There can be only one height of a given circle, for there can be no two absolutely identical segments of a line. Having assumed, however, that the world lacks a definite fixed center, any point within it can be regarded as both its highest and its lowest point. This paradoxical consequence is neatly brought out in Prince John's comment on the Cardinal's reasoning:

> I understand; and the situation is as you say it is. And so, as regards what is [perfectly] round, neither what is outermost nor what is innermost can be seen, since both are [one and] the same atom. Now, whatever is present in a [perfect] sphere or in something [perfectly] round is both outermost and innermost; and so, neither the roundness nor any part of the roundness can be seen. Nevertheless, I do not say that a round thing cannot be seen. Rather, the roundness of the thing is invisible; as regards true roundness, nothing is visible. Therefore, when sight judges something to be round, there is not true roundness in that thing.[6]

Thus it is not possible to see the roundness of the Universe, even though the things contained within it are perfectly visible. The Universe is in fact paradoxical in its essence: it is both infinitely great and infinitely small: it is infinitely great for no boundaries in space can be found to delimit its greatness; it is infinitely small, for being an indivisible unit it is like a point than which nothing smaller can exist. This unity of opposite attributes characterizing the Universe's essence proves that it is the image of the Absolute Maximum, which is no other than God.[7]

The reference to God as "simple and absolute Maximum" is meant to emphasize His supremacy and transcendence in all conceivable orders; it is a development of St. Anselm's of Canterbury idea that God must be conceived as a "being, than which no greater can be thought."[8] Absolute Maximum is the most perfect and precise Equality, which is not subject to further gradation or alteration, therefore can take as the first principle of all "measurement," that is as the absolute basis of the identity of all things that can be more or less beautiful, good, equal, etc. For this reason, the Absolute Maximum is at the same time the Absolute Minimum since it constitutes the essence of every single thing as its necessary ultimate and simplest element. Cusanus's classical formulations on the coincidence of the Maximum and the Minimum, the celebrated coincidence of opposites, are found in his *On Learned Ignorance*:

> Hence, since the absolutely Maximum is all that which can be, it is altogether actual. And just as there cannot be a greater, so for the same reason there cannot be a lesser, since it is all that which can be. But the Minimum is that than which there cannot be a lesser. And since the Maximum is also such, it is evident that the Minimum coincides with the Maximum. (...) Therefore, opposing features belong only to those things which can be comparatively greater and lesser; they befit these things in different ways; [but they do] not at all [befit] the absolutely Maximum, since it is beyond all opposition. Therefore, because the absolutely Maximum is absolutely and actually all things which can be (and is so free of all opposition that the Minimum coincides with it), it is beyond both all affirmation and all negation.[9]

The Maximum and Minimum are descriptions Nicholas applies to God; he also applies to God such names as Absolute Entity, and Pure Actuality, that is a reality, which actually is all that, which It can be. All created things, that is all things other than God, not only have actuality of their own but also contain the element of potentiality, which encompasses all that, which they have not yet become and also that which they will never realize. God is the only reality, that really and actually is all that, which He can be. This feature is expressed by the name *Possest*:

> For let us agree that [there is a single] word [which] signifies by a very simple signification as much as [is signified by] the compound expression "Possibility exists" ("posse est")—meaning that possibility itself exists. Now, because what exists, exists actually: the possibility-to-be exists insofar as the possibility-to-be is actual. Suppose we call this possest [i.e., Actualized-possibility]. All things are enfolded in it [i.e., in Actualized-possibility]; and ["Actualized-possibility"] is a sufficiently approximate name for God, according to our human concept of Him.[10]

In another of his works, Nicholas refers to God with the name *Non-Aliud* in order to emphasize His perfect identity with Himself (in contrast to all beings other than God, which are not perfectly identical with themselves because always crucially related to other entities) and the fact that He is the Absolute and only totally non-conditioned beginning of all things.[11] These novel names and descriptions applied to God, seemingly involving inner contradiction, fulfilled a definite didactic function with respect to God's nature: they exploded easy, anthropomorphic conceptions of God, compelled the readers to revise their schematic representations of the Divine Reality and opened the way for an insight into the paradoxical nature of the Absolute, which cannot be measured by human thinking.[12] What from the human limited point of view seems to imply a contradiction, in God forms a higher unity and harmony. God, when seen from the human perspective, appears to be a paradox, an identity of aspects, which in our experience are irreducibly opposed to one another. To this paradox, apparent in human thinking about God, Cusanus gave the name of "coincidence of opposites," and he thought of human intelligence as inherently separated from the adequate vision of God by an insurmountable barrier, which he referred to as a wall of paradise, paradise being the condition of intellect allowing unhindered contemplation of the divine reality, from which human intellect is barred in its present state.[13] Yet the paradoxes inherent in human efforts to grasp the reality of God and express the knowledge of God in an adequate language play a vital propaedeutic and anagogical role: they make us realize the inadequacy of our comprehension of the supreme reality and the metaphoric nature of our statements about God and thus prepare ourselves for a future vision of God, which will be simple and free from all apparent contradictions.

Nicholas also knew the famous traditional description of God as an "intelligible sphere, whose centre is everywhere and circumference nowhere," which he may have found in Alain of Lille and his *Rules of theology* or *Sermon on the intelligible sphere*; as we have seen, he also applied this description to the Universe as a whole.[14]

Every thing that is seen as round is more or less so, for it is only round by virtue of participation in the perfect or absolute roundness than which nothing can be more round. Nor is the roundness of the Universe this maximum roundness, even though it is the greatest roundness in actual existence; the roundness of the world is like the one of any other round object but an image of the perfect roundness, which in its essence is the same as eternity:

> For the round world is not roundness itself, than which there can be no greater roundness, but [is a roundness] than which there is not actually a greater. However, absolute roundness is not of the nature

of the world's roundness but is the cause and exemplar of the world's roundness. I call absolute roundness eternity; the world's roundness is an image of eternity. For in a circle—in which there is no beginning or end, since in it there is no point that is a beginning rather than an end—I see the image of eternity. Therefore, I assert that [the world's] roundness is the image of eternity, since [absolute] roundness and eternity are the same thing.[15]

Infinity and eternity turn out to be two of the ways in which the Universe reflects and expresses the Absolute Divine Maximum. This statement introduces into the discussion the problem of eternity of the world, much in the debate from the 13th century onward. Even ecclesiastical authorities felt obliged to intervene in the crisis by condemning a number of supposedly heterodox theses, and they did so, most notably on 7 March 1277.[16] Nicholas of Cusa must have been aware of these developments and of later polemics with the so-called Latin Averroism, yet he approached the problem of eternity of the world from a different perspective, namely starting from assumptions, which were much closer to Plato's *Timaeus* than to Aristotelian physics.

He observed, that it is legitimate and right to call the world eternal, however, not because it lacks a beginning but because it is derived from and participates in eternity, which is the foundation and condition of its very existence. Nor can it be legitimately maintained that God existed before the creation, for time, with the "before" and "after," came into being only with the creation of the world:

For it is not possible that something existed but that time did not yet exist, since "existed" is indicative of past time. Time is eternity's creature; for time is not eternity, which is present as a whole at once, but is the image of eternity, since it consists of successiveness.[17]

Cusanus's concept of eternity was clearly related to the notion found in Plato's *Timaeus* and in Calcidius's commentary on that dialogue. According to that concept, eternity is duration without any succession of instants, in a changeless "now," without any past or future; by contrast, time is duration consisting of successive moments. According to Timaeus, time is the image of eternity, and Cardinal wholly endorses this conception:

We conceive of eternity only in terms of duration. We cannot at all imagine duration apart from successiveness. Hence, successiveness, which is temporal duration, presents itself whenever we attempt to conceive of eternity. But our mind tells us that absolute duration, which is eternity, naturally precedes successive duration. And so, by means of successive duration, as by means of an image, duration-in-itself, free from successiveness, is seen—even as truth [is seen] by means of its image.[18]

Being the image and copy of true eternity, which is immutable fullness of being, time can nevertheless be called eternal in a qualified sense, as it has had no beginning in time. With even more reason, the qualification of "eternal" can be attributed to the Universe since it directly derives from true Eternity without the mediation of time, while time only flows from Eternity via the intermediary of the world. In allowing for the material Universe to be described as eternal, Cusanus, in a way, takes sides in the Scholastic controversy concerning eternity of the world:

> For the world did not begin in time. For not time, but only Eternity, preceded the world. Thus, time, too, is sometimes spoken of as eternal (as the Prophet speaks of "eternal time"), since time did not have a beginning in time. For time did not precede time, but [only] Eternity did. Therefore, time is called eternal because it flows from Eternity. Similarly, the world is also eternal because it is derived from Eternity and not from time. But it befits the world, more than it befits time, to be given the name eternal, since the duration of the world does not depend on time. For if the motion of the heavens and if time (which is the measure of motion) were to cease, there would not cease to be a world. On the other hand, if the world were completely to perish, time would cease. Therefore, it befits the world, more than it befits time, that it be called eternal.[19]

Possibly Cusanus's conception of the relationship obtaining between eternity, the Universe and time owed some of its inspiration to Boethius, who insisted on eternity as the mode of existence characteristic of and peculiar to God. In his *Consolation of Philosophy*, Boethius defines eternity as infinite "now" and in his theological opuscules as "total and simultaneous possession of interminable life."[20] The Universe, being an image of God's unique way of existence, also takes some part in the absolute eternity, just as its rounded form is a copy of God's absolute and perfect Roundness.

God's eternity is not only the durable basis for the changeable duration of the Universe but it is also the creative power that gives form to the created matter of the world "in accordance with the altogether free will of the altogether perfect God."[21] The actually existing world is not absolutely perfect; in fact, both a more and a less perfect worlds could have been created, and we know of no reason why God, "in accordance with His altogether free will," should have chosen this rather than any other possible world. What we know, however, is that this world eternally existed as a pure possibility in God's intellect, and this possibility

came to be realized in actual existence. The act by which God brought
the actually existing world into real being was far from exhausting His
infinite capacity for creative action. Consideration of human productive
art can allow us to get some insight into God's Creative Art:

> Accordingly, from this likeness with the human art you know how
> you can, to some extent, make surmises about the Divine Creative
> Art, although between God's creating and man's producing there is as
> much difference as between the Creator and the creature. Therefore,
> because within itself the Divine Mind conceives of the world, the
> Divine Mind is called the Archetypal World. (This [Divine] Concept
> is the Divine Mind, which is equal to the Concept.) Now, God willed
> to manifest, and make visible, the beauty of His Concept. He created
> the possibility, or the capability, of a beautiful world's being made.
> And He created the motion through which the world was derived
> from possibility, so that there was made this visible world, in which
> the possibility-of-there-being-a-world is such as God willed it to be
> and such as it was able actually to be determined to be.[22]

God is the unique and universal cause of all things other than Himself: He is the efficient, formal and final cause both of the Universe as a
whole and of every single creature within that Universe. This world of
ours exists eternally in God's Intellect as an archetype; it exists there as
integrated within the perfect Unity of God's essence, in the form that
is "compressed and involved." The world, so far as it exists as an archetypal exemplar in the eternity of God's mind, is not subject to any
change or evolution, nor does it come into being in successive stages in
time. For this world of our experience to come into being on its own, another principle was necessary to fulfil the function of the material cause.
Matter, strictly speaking, is no real cause; it cannot be one for it is not
capable of actual existence on its own. Matter only comes into being as
an element of created things; it is nothing but a pure possibility, capabil-
ity of becoming something and the principle of changeability; as such, it
is a metaphysically necessary condition of real things coming into being,
although it cannot be said that matter exists before things, as, according
to Nicholas, this would involve contradiction. Thus, Cusanus wholly
approves of the traditional doctrine of creation out of nothing, as the
following passage makes evident:

> Therefore, matter is not something actually existent; rather, a thing
> that is made is said to be made from matter because it was able to be
> made. For the Divine Mind would not be omnipotent if it could make
> something only from something else—a feat which a created mind,
> which is not at all omnipotent, does every day.[23]

He is also in perfect agreement with the traditional doctrine in holding that the structure of the created Universe in its unity and triplicity constitutes an image of God, which represents a reduced development of the Trinitarian *oikonomia*.[24] This threefold unity of the Universe is realized within the metaphysical framework of the four universal modes of existence, the doctrine of the four modes of existence Cusanus took from the thought of Thierry of Chartres and first developed in his *On Learned Ignorance*. In this work, he wrote as follows:

> Therefore, the oneness of the universe is three, since it is from possibility, connecting necessity, and union-which can be called possibility, actuality, and union. And here from infer four universal modes of being. There is the mode of being which is called Absolute Necessity, according as God is Form of forms, Being of beings, and Essence (*ratio*) or Quiddity of things. With regard to this mode of being: in God all things are Absolute Necessity itself. Another mode [of being] is according as things exist in the connecting necessity; in this necessity, just as in a mind, the forms-of-things, true in themselves, exist with a distinction, and an order, of nature. We shall see later whether this is so. Another mode of being is according as, in determined possibility, things are actually this or that. And the lowest mode of being is according as things are possible to be, and it is absolute possibility.[25]

According to this metaphysical scheme of the four modes of existing adopted by Nicholas, the Universe exists as a determined possibility (*possibilitas determinata*) between Absolute Necessity (*necessitas absoluta*), which is God Himself, the reduced form of necessity which is the necessity of the complex order of nature (*necessitas complexionis*), which determines the laws regulating the functioning of the actually created Universe on the one side and an absolute possibility (*possibilitas absoluta*) of matter considered in total abstraction from actually existing beings on the other.[26]

These four modes of being constitute a framework which enables a precise definition of the relationship between the divine transcendence and immanence. In this context, it is important to stress that by invoking the concept of Absolute Necessity, Cusanus does not mean to question or diminish God's absolute freedom; all he intends is to exclude from God's existence and activity the element of chance and contingency. As a proof of his commitment to the theory of God's perfect freedom, let us quote once again his statement from *The Bowling Game* (I, 19) that the world was made according to "altogether free will of an altogether perfect God." This combination of perfect freedom and perfect comprehension of the universality of things makes it meaningful to speak of the Divine Providence, which would be unthinkable if God did not possess a necessary knowledge of all things.

In his book *The Kingdom and the Glory*, Giorgio Agamben presents on the basis of impressively large historical material two "political paradigms," whose roots can be shown to derive from Christian theology: (1) "political theology, which founds the transcendence of sovereign over on the single God" and (2) "economic theology, which replaces this transcendence with the idea of an *oikonomia*, conceived as an immanent ordering – domestic and not political in a strict sense – of both divine and human life."[27] The proponents of the latter paradigm typically refer to the idea of Divine Providence as the factor carrying into effect the project of the Divine *oikonomia*. Agamben claims,

> Providence (the government) is that through which theology and philosophy try to come to terms with the splitting of classical ontology into two separate realities: being and praxis, transcendent and immanent good, theology and *oikonomia*. Providence presents itself as a machine aimed at joining back together the two fragments in *gubernatio dei*, the divine government of the world.[28]

Quoting from Chrisippus and Alexander of Afrodisias, but above all from Boethius, Agamben takes up the discussion of the problem of the relationship between Providence and Fate, the latter being conceived as the force executing the decrees of Providence through the agency of secondary causes. He represents the relation of Providence to Fate in terms of the cooperation of the legislative and executive powers in a political system:

> In other words, the governmental machine functions like an incessant theodicy, in which the Kingdom of providence legitimates and founds the Government of fate, and the latter guarantees the order that the former has established and renders it operative.[29]

In Cusanus's representation of the Divine *oikonomia*, God, who is the Absolute Maximum and Absolute Necessity (the aspects that form His transcendence), is also the power that is present to every particular entity within the world giving it the necessary support for its existence and thriving (which is what His immanence means). An unusually graphic illustration of the interplay between the Divine transcendence and immanence as two aspects of God's providential government of the world is found in *The Vision of God*, in which the reader, together with the monks of the abbey of Tegernsee, is put in the presence of the icon of the All-seeing Face:

> 0 Lord, by a certain sense-experience I now behold, in this image of You, Your providence. For if You do not desert me, who am the least of all men, then You will never desert anyone. You are present to each

and every thing—just as being, without which things cannot exist, is present to each and every thing. For You who are the Absolute Being of all things are present to each thing as if You were concerned about no other thing at all. (...) For You, O Lord, behold each existing thing in such way that no existing thing can conceive that You have any other concern than (1) that this very thing exist in the best manner it can and (2) that all other existing things exist only in order to serve the following end: viz., that this thing upon which you are looking exist in the best way.[30]

In 0order adequately to elucidate God's causal relationship to the world, Cusanus used the technical vocabulary he found in Thierry of Chartres, and in particular the pair of correlated terms *complicatio-explicatio*.[31] God, in His Absolute Necessity or Providence, contains in a "compressed" or "complicated" way, the whole of created reality, which, once made to exist on its own and outside God's Intellect, develops in bringing out all the details, which were implicitly contained in the providential vision according to the established necessary laws of nature (*necessitas complexionis*) and producing the particular entities comprising the world (*possibilitas determinata*), which in a perceptible form represent plenty of ways in which matter (*possibilitas absoluta*) can be shaped in order to form the world of concrete individuals. The created world as a whole, the "explication" of the intelligible world "complicated" in the Divine Providence and each and every being contained therein are all manifestations of their Triune Source. Cusanus develops this theme in *The Bowling Game*:

> Therefore, if we look at the one universe's plurality of creatures, we find in these creatures oneness (which is the being of them all) and equality-of-oneness. For in equal measure they all have being, since one being is neither more a being nor less a being than is another. In each and every being, being as a whole is present in equal measure. And the reason all beings are united into one is that in each and every being there is the union-of-being-and-of-equality that proceeds from oneness and from equality. In this way you see that the First Cause is one because it is First and is trine because it is Oneness, Equality, and Union. And unless this statement were true, the First Cause would not be the Being of beings. Therefore, God, because He is the Creator, can be only trine and one. Hence, there exists a created world in order that in the world the trine and one Creator may be seen.[32]

The basic metaphysical property of all created things is their dependence on their ultimate cause, that is on God: their being (*esse*) is *ab-esse*, that is "being-from," a derivative way of being, which is the only way of existence they are capable of having when constituted on their own, outside the Divine Mind. God is the truth of each and every thing, the Absolute Essence (*quidditas absoluta*) of every entity, and the being of a created thing itself reduces in fact to being an image, reflection or manifestation of the perfect being of the Creator. Whatever a finite mind perceives is nothing but a particular appearance of the very *Posse Ipsum*:

> Moreover, observe what the mind sees in different beings, which are not anything except what they are possible to be and which can have only what-they-have-from-Possibility. And you will see that different beings are only different modes of the manifestation of Possibility but that their [ultimate] Quiddity cannot be different, because it is Possibility itself, which is manifested in different ways.[33]

One could say, using a term characteristically used in the intellectual tradition dear to Nicholas, that of Pseudo-Dionysius, Maximus the Confessor and Eriugena, that the created world is in its essence divine theophany. The conception of the world as theophany assumes is that since it is not possible for our finite minds immediately to see God in His essence, God reveals Himself and His mysteries to human beings through the intermediary of the creation. Creation functions as a sign, symbol and a meaningful structure, whose role is to point to their Cause and manifest Its attributes. This conception was concisely expressed by St. Paul in his Letter to Romans: *The invisible things of Him, including His eternal power and divinity, are clearly seen from the creation of the world, by means of understanding created things* (Rom 1, 20).[34] Theophany is like a light, whose brightness cannot be directly perceived as it is in itself but can only be seen through the intermediary of things it illuminates and thus makes visible. Visible light is a good illustration and a fitting symbol both of the Divine transcendence and immanence: when at its most intense, it remains inaccessible to human perception, yet it makes all things visible and in these things becomes visible itself. In a like way, God manifests Himself in created things as the supreme source of their reality and cognoscibility:

> Therefore, Possibility itself is called Light by some saints—not perceptible light or rational light or intelligible light but the Light of all things that can give light—since nothing can possibly be brighter or clearer or more beautiful than Possibility. Therefore, look unto perceptible light, without which there cannot be perceptual seeing; and note that in every color and in everything visible there is no

other basis than light, which appears in differing ways in the different modes-of-being of the colors. And note that if light is removed, then neither color nor anything visible nor [any] seeing can remain. But the clearness of light, insofar as light exists in itself, transcends visual power. Therefore, light is not seen as it is, but, rather, it is manifested in things visible (...). Light manifests itself in visible things not in order to show itself as visible but, rather, in order to manifest itself as invisible, since its clarity cannot be grasped in visible things.[35]

Every particular thing within the Universe and the Universe as a whole represent God, each in its own unique way, according to its own degree of contraction (*contractio*). The degree of contraction proper to a given thing is the measure by which the perfection of the Absolute Essence is diminished in the essence of that thing. Every individual thing has its own unique degree of contraction which means that it represents the Absolute Essence, in its own unique way. The degree of contraction of a given thing is in fact the metaphysical principle which constitutes the unique identity of that thing. Since the Absolute Essence is present contractedly in the Universe as a whole and in every single thing within it, it is true to say that every single thing in the world represents and mirrors every other thing, including God and the Universe itself. In other words, Anaxagoras was right in claiming that "each thing is in each thing":

From Book One it is evident that God is in all things in such way that all things are in Him; and it is now evident [from II, 4] that God is in all things through the mediation of the universe, as it were. Hence, it is evident that all is in all and each in each.[36]

The work *On Learned Ignorance* comprises three books, each devoted to one of the three designates of the term maximum. The first book discusses Maximum in the simple and absolute sense, which is God; the second the contracted Maximum, that is the Universe, which is a unity, yet existent in and dependent on plurality; and the third treats of the Maximum which is both absolute and contracted; this third and paradoxical Maximum is a man and God in one person: Jesus Christ.[37] The person of Jesus Christ appears in the dialogue *The Bowling-Game*; it is made into a centerpiece of the whole discussion: Jesus Christ is said to be the purpose and the reward of the game of life. This clearly shows that Christology is the keystone of the whole system of Cusanus's thought; it provides the synthesis that brings together his concerns with the theology of the transcendent God and cosmology as the contracted manifestation of God.

However, a discovery of Christ as the ultimate end of the game of life requires first of all a comprehension and assimilation of the presuppositions and rules of that game. It takes an intelligent player to grasp the meaning and importance of the game we are engaged in playing, just as the proper reading and interpretation of the theophanies and symbols present in the world calls for a sensitive and comprehending reader. Without the human rational player-reader, both the sense of the game and the value of the world will remain undiscovered.

Notes

1   LG I, 6, p. 1184.
2   Cf. DERMOT MORAN. *Nicholas of Cusa and modern philosophy*, in: The Cambridge Companion to Renaissance Philosophy, ed. J. Hankins, Cambridge University Press, Cambridge, 2007, pp. 175–176. See a different opinion of Hans Blumenberg: HANS BLUMENBERG. *The Legitimacy of the Modern Age*, The MIT Press, Cambridge, MA, 1985, pp. 503–504.
3   DI II, 11, 156–157, p. 90.
4   DI II, 11, 161, p. 92.
5   Cf. WILHELM DUPRÉ. "Docte ignorance (thème)," in: *Encyclopédie des mystiques rhénans*. D'Eckhart à Nicolas de Cues et leur réception, ed. M.-A. Vannier, Cerf, Paris, 2011, pp. 394–400.
6   LG I, 11, p. 1186.
7   Cf. JEAN-MICHEL COUNET. *Matématiques et dialectique chez Nicolas de Cues*, Librairie Vrin, Paris, 2000, pp. 247–250.
8   ANSELM of CANTERUBRY. *Proslogion* 2, tr. by J. Hopkins and H. Richardson, in: *Complete Philosophical and Theological Treatises of Anselm of Canterbury*, The Arthur J. Banning Press, Minneapolis, 2000, p. 93 (proslogion.pdf [jasper-hopkins.info']): "Therefore, O Lord, You who give understanding to faith, grant me to understand – to the degree You know to be advantageous – that You exist, as we believe, and that You are what we believe [You to be]. Indeed, we believe You to be something than which nothing greater can be thought." Cf. BRIAN DAVIS. "Anselm and the ontological argument." in: *The Cambridge Companion to Anselm*, eds. B. Davies, B. Leftow, Cambridge University Press, Cambridge, 2004, p. 159.
9   DI I, IV, 11–12, p. 9.
10 DP 14, pp. 77–79. Cf. PETER J. CASARELLA. "Nicholas of Cusa and the Power of the Possible." *American Catholic Philosophical Quarterly*, 64, n. 1, 1990, pp. 7–34.
11 NA 7, p. 1111; Cf. SILVIANNE ASPRAY. "Performative Finitude: Theological Language and the God-World Relationship in Nicholas of Cusa 'De Non Aliud'." *International Journal of Systematic Theology*, 24, n. 2, 2022, p. 174.
12 Cf. RICHARD MARK SAINSBURY. *Paradoxes*, 3rd edition, Cambridge University Press, Cambridge, 2009, p. 1. Cf. CLYDE L. MILLER. *Reading Cusanus. Metaphor and Dialectic in a Conjectural Universe,* The Catholic University of America Press, Washington D.C., 2003, pp. 133–139.
13 Cf. VD12, 51, p. 703; 13, 53, p. 704. Cf. GIANLUCA CUOZZO. "Coincidence des opposes," in: *Encyclopédie des mystiques rhénans. D'Eckhart à Nicolas de Cues et leur réception*, ed. M.-A. Vannier, Cerf, Paris, 2011, pp. 253–257.

14 Cf. ALAIN DE LILLE. *Règles de théologie* 7, ed. F. Hudry, Les Éditions du Cerf, Paris, 1995, pp. 109–111; cf. BLUMENBERG. *The Legitimacy*, p. 491.
15 LG I, 16, p. 1189.
16 Cf. FERNAND VAN STEENBERGHEN. *La philosophie au XIIIe siècle*, Publications Universitaires, Louvain, Béatrice-Nauwelaerts, Paris, 1966, p. 483 and f.; FRANCOIS-XAVIER PUTALLAZ. "Censorship," in: *The Cambridge History of Medieval Philosophy*, eds. R. Pasnau, Ch. Van Dyke, vol. 1, Cambridge University Press, Cambridge, 2010, pp. 100–105.
17 LG II, 87, p. 1228.
18 LG II, 88, p. 1228. Cf. CALCIDIUS. *On Plato's "Timaeus"* 105, tr. by J. Magee, Harvard University Press, Cambridge, MA, London, 2016, p. 297.
19 LG I, 18, p. 1190.
20 Cf. BOETHIUS. *Consolation of Philosophy* V, 6, trans. Joel C. Relihan, Hackett Publishing Company, Indianapolis, Cambridge, 2001, p. 144.
21 LG I, 19, p. 1190.
22 LG I, 45, p. 1204.
23 LG I, 46, p. 1205.
24 DI II, 128, p. 76.
25 DI II, 130, p. 77. Cf. DAVID ALBERTSON. *Mathematical Theologies. Nicholas of Cusa and the Legacy of Thierry of Chartres*, Oxford University Press, Oxford, 2014, pp. 171, 268–273.
26 Cf. THIERRY OF CHARTRES. *Commentaries on Boethius by Thierry of Chartres and His School*, ed. N. M. Häring, Pontifical Institute of Mediaeval Studies, Toronto 1971, pp. 157–161, 164–165, 271, 272, 275.
27 AGAMBEN GIORGIO. *The Kingdom and the Glory*, trans. by L. Chiesa, M. Mandarni, Stanford University Press, Stanford, 2011, p. 1.
28 There, p. 140; cf. p. 113.
29 There, p. 129.
30 VD IV, 10, p. 684.
31 Cf. THIERRY OF CHARTRES. *Commentaries on Boethius by Thierry of Chartres and His School*, ed. N. M. Häring, Pontifical Institute of Mediaeval Studies, Toronto, 1971, p. 174. Cf. AGNIESZKA KIJEWSKA. "Scot Erigéne et Nicolas dc Cues: *processio et explicatio*." in : *Noesis. Revue philosophique du Centre de recherche d'histoire des idées*, 26-27, 2016-2017: *Nicolas de Cues (1401-1464). Le tournant anthroplogique de la philosophie*, Université de Nice-Sophia Antipolis pp. 105–111.
32 LG II, 83, p. 1126.
33 AT 9, p. 1427.
34 DP 2, p. 63; Cf. AGNIESZKA KIJEWSKA. "Latin Neoplatonism. The Medieval Period," in: *The Oxford Handbook of Roman Philosophy*, eds. M. Garani, D. Konstan, G. Reydams-Schils, Oxford University Press, Oxford, 2023, pp. 570–571; cf. NANCY J. HUDSON. *Becoming God*. The Doctrine of Theosis in Nicholas of Cusa, The Catholic University of America Press, Washington, D.C., 2007, pp. 45–88.
35 AT 8, pp. 1426–1427.
36 DI II, V, 117, p. 71.
37 DI I, II, 6–7, pp. 6–7.

7 The circle of values

At the start of the discussion in *The Bowling Game*, the Cardinal observes that "no small amount of philosophy" is signified by the arrangements and rules of the game of bowls. At the end of Book Two of that dialogue, Prince Albert, the Cardinal's interlocutor, asks for a summary of the debate to "make this discussion valuable and memorable," to which the Cardinal responds:

> I will try. But there does not occur to me a way in which I may better make valuable (*valere*) what I have said that if I speak about value (*valor*).[1]

Further on, the Prince suggests a narrowing down of the topic of the discussion to matters related to value and price:

> I think that if you were to limit your discourse to [the topic of] the price of value (*pretium valoris*), you would instruct us the more greatly. *Cardinal*: Perhaps you mean [for me] to speak about money (*pecunia*). *Albert*: Yes, I want [you] to.[2]

Thus, the basic categories of economics – value, price and money – enter into the discussion and become the means through which the elucidation of the moral and spiritual matters of most importance will be sought. The term value, which in contemporary philosophical language is used in the most general sense of good, goodness, in medieval usage was restricted to economic context. Generally, it can be said that medieval theories of value (or of what we would term value) developed in two different areas of concern. One area was that of general metaphysics and the theory of transcendental properties of being as such; one of these transcendentals was the property of goodness/good (*bonum*): the medieval theory conceived of being as inherently good or valuable. The other area of concern was strictly economic: it was introduced into medieval intellectual debate, thanks to the reception of Aristotelianism, and

DOI: 10.4324/9781003310693-7

in particular *Nicomachean Ethics*, which discussed such topics as value of goods in the context of trade and market exchange and the problem of just price. A valuable contribution to the medieval economic debate was made by Thomas Aquinas, who generalized the notion of price (*pretium*) and introduced the concept of economic value.[3]

As far as the former, metaphysical discussion of the good and goodness in the Middle Ages is concerned, it had been inspired by Boethius, who in his *opuscula sacra*, following the ideas of St. Augustine, asserted that the properties of goodness and unity to be coextensive with being.[4] This seminal insight came to full fruition only in the 13th century, when, under the impact of the newly discovered Aristotelianism, medieval metaphysics took mature shape as a *scientia transcendens*, that is science considering the properties belonging to reality as such and inseparable from being as being in all its categorial forms. Being, unity, truth, good and beauty were most often cited as universal properties of being, usually referred to as transcendentals; the classical theory of transcendentals was produced by St. Thomas Aquinas,[5] but there were also other rival theories. All medieval theories of transcendentals unanimously asserted good to be an inseparable property of being, a point which necessarily followed from the conception of God's universal causality: since all things were made by God, who is Absolute Good, all things must be necessarily and inherently good. God is Good itself, and perfectly knowing Himself, He has the exemplar of Good in His Intellect; thus, Good is primarily an eternal and immutable idea in Divine Mind. Creations are all good only in a secondary sense, yet they must be thought as good insofar as they are participations in, reflections of, and unfolding of the cosmos inherent in Divine Intellect.

It will be useful for our discussion to quote here the interesting observations of Roman Ingarden on the philosophical conceptions of value. The object of his comments is the theory of Max Scheler, nevertheless his remarks on the way values come to be realized in the world of our experience, may be helpful in our efforts to follow Cusanus's thought:

Plato, as we know, considered values to be so called 'ideas', that is certain extra-temporal, unchangeable entities – 'ideal' entities, as we say today. In the twentieth century, Max Scheler believed that values are 'ideas', or ideal objects and claimed that one can attain to a mathematical type of a priori knowledge of them. Alongside 'values' he also acknowledged 'goods' [*Güter*], i.e. certain individual (real) objects to which values were somehow supposed to accrue. (...) we could say that a 'value', in the sense employed in this paper, is that ensemble of moments, which in appearing in a particular object brings it about that this object is not simply some thing, but that it is precisely a 'good' in Scheler's sense. These moments are

individual, and possibly have their correlates in ideas of ideal qualities, but as entities they are just as different from these correlates as
the shape of a square appearing concretely on a particular thing is
different from the geometrical 'idea' of a square or the ideal quality
'squareness'.[6]

Essential to the comprehension of Nicholas's conception of values is
Plato's theory mentioned in the quoted passage, according to which values
are "'ideas', that is certain extra-temporal, unchangeable entities – 'ideal'
entities." In a truly Platonic fashion, Cusanus affirmed that (1) the objective ground for the reality of values is their presence in the "essence of
value" eternally existent in God's Mind. Scholars are not unanimous on
whether Cusanus endorsed the classical formulation of the doctrine of exemplarism, which presupposed a certain plurality of ideas in God's Mind
(Kurt Flasch), or whether he replaced it with his own formulation.[7] It appears that Cusanus's position on the problem of how values are grounded
in Divine Intellect was fairly original: Divine Mind, being free of any plurality or division, is the objective foundation of the values inherent in
things; it is the universal measure, precision and truth of all things; it is
also "the concept of concepts," the simple Absolute Essence which is present a *priori* in the minds of humans and enables them correctly to judge
about the value of things they encounter in their experience.[8]

(2) Individual things in the world of human experience, which in their
totality form the unfolding of the Absolute Essence and Exemplary Value,
have certain properties, which reveal and represent their value, internal as
well as external.[9] To use Ingarden's words, we might say that these properties are constituted by "that ensemble of moments, which in appearing
in a particular object brings it about that this object is not simply some
thing, but that it is precisely a 'good'"; moreover "these moments are individual, and possibly have their correlates in ideas of ideal qualities, but as
entities they are [...] different from these correlates." One might also say
that goodness/value found in concrete objects of human everyday experience forms the meeting point between the divine transcendence and immanence. (3) The features of individual things which constitute their value,
and which are the unfolding of the Value as such (the objective side of the
cognitive relationship), would remain vain and inefficient unless recognized and appreciated as valuable by a competent perceiver; thus, another
condition for the appearance of values in the world is human cognition
and appreciation of them (the subjective side of the cognitive relationship).

Nicholas of Cusa sought to illuminate the complex situation of value
appearing as objectified in things of the world, and then being recognized and adopted in practice by human beings, through considering
an analogous situation taken from economic practice, namely the one
involving money, its coining, its managing and use. (4) He gave an

additional, theological dimension to that analogy by charging money, the carrier of economic value, with religious symbolism: a coin is said to be an image of Christ, the incarnate Divine Power and the Divine Currency, which man must properly interpret, just as one interprets the images and inscriptions on a coin and "put into circulation." As Devin Singh in his book *Divine Currency* remarks,

> Money serves as a useful point of entry into such considerations because it brings to the fore questions about the materialization of transcendent value and the role of representation, issues central to debates about God's relation to the world, for instance; because it crystallizes certain relations of power, authority, and control present in economic exchange which are critical to discussions of divine sovereignty; and because it offers a discrete set of attributes to analyse within the expansive field of economics, providing a workable scope of inquiry. (...) Money is also a mark of obligation to this power, for monetary economy is set into motion by taxation.[10]

Thus, according to this author, the essential property of money, which renders it a useful vehicle for religious meanings and concepts, is their ability to make materially present and operative the power of the sovereign authority which has instituted them; Devin Singh calls this aspect of money "monetary incarnation." Through the agency of money, the sovereign authority can influence and shape the society it rules.[11]

Nicholas ingeniously makes use of various aspects of "monetary incarnation," in order to present his own conception of the complex relationship obtaining between God, the world and human mind. Most importantly, the symbol of money, that is an object charged with value, makes it clear that what is at stake in the game of life is something most desirable and worthy of possession, that the purpose of human efforts is some irreplaceable gain.[12]

Now let us take a look at Cusanus's text in the light of the above points.

Exemplarism was a common doctrine of all theological writers of Cusanus's time; we have referred to his own version of it more than once in the above. God, the unique, universal and intelligent cause of the created reality, contains in His Intellect archetypal models of all things. This archetypal Universe exists in God in the way God exists, that is as eternally identical with Divine Essence, without any plurality and division; it is only when incarnate in matter that the divine ideas produce plurality of individuals. The Cardinal explains this to Prince Albert in the following way:

> And it is not necessary that because of the plurality of exemplifications there be also a plurality of exemplars, since a single exemplar

suffices for an infinite number of exemplifications. For the exemplar naturally precedes its exemplification. And prior to all plurality there is oneness, which is the exemplar of the entire exemplifying multitude.[13]

Thus, there is only one supreme model for all reality, imitated and copied in a plurality of ways, just as there is only one supreme Value, whose unfolding and resplendence are particular individual things. The unfolding of all that is contained in the divine exemplar takes place according to a definite order, which is one and simple when seen from God's perspective, although appears as multiple and complex in the perception of a finite cognizing subject.[14]

Since, of necessity, there is an ordering of all the works of God (...), the ordering can neither exist nor be understood to exist without a beginning, a middle, and an end. Now, [this order—viz., of beginning, middle, and end—] is a most perfect and most simple Order, than which there can be no order that is more perfect or more simple. It is present in everything that is ordered, and in it all ordered things are present—present in the way in which we premised in the general proposition at the outset [of our discussion]. But in this Order, which is the Exemplar of all orders, it is necessary that the Middle be most simple, since the Order is most simple. Therefore, the Middle will be so equal that it will be Equality itself. This Order cannot be understood by us by means of any other distinguishing than by means of a most well-ordered progression that begins with oneness and ends with the number three.[15]

So, unity and triplicity are the most elementary forms in which the divine simplicity and necessity is constituted and expressed, and derivative unity and triplicity form the mark necessarily present in each and every created entity. This mark is reproduced and transmitted at every stage of the progression, by which the simplicity and necessity of the unique Divine Exemplar, which is the first and absolute Unity and Trinity, passes into the plurality of created things contained within the unity of the Universe and subject to ordering determined by the laws imitating the supreme Order of the Trinity.

Every created entity imitates and in this way represents the Supreme Exemplar in its own unique manner, which is the same thing as participation in the Absolute Value. Nicholas is a resolute upholder of the essential uniqueness of every individual thing: every particular thing imitates and represents in a diminished way the Divine Essence, yet no two things in the world imitate and represent the Absolute Essence in exactly the same way, although all created things equally receive from God not only their proper degree of being but also their own measure of value:

> Being is something good and noble and precious. And so, whatever exists is not devoid of value. For nothing can at all exist that does not have some value. Nor can there be found to be anything that is of least value, so that it could not be of lesser value; nor is anything of such great value that it could not be of greater value. However, only value that is the Value of values and that is present in all things valuable, and in which [all] things valuable are present, enfolds within itself all value and cannot be more or less valuable. Therefore, conceive of this Absolute Value, which is the Cause of all value, as concealed [symbolically] in the center of all the circles [in our game]. And make the outermost circle to be farthest from value and to be almost of no value; and consider how it is that, by means of a triune progression unto ten, value is increased in the manner that has often been mentioned; and, [thereupon], you will enter into a delicious speculation.[16]

This passage shows once again the way the ground prepared for playing the game of bowls depicts the relationship obtaining between God, the fullness of all value and the hierarchically ordered world sharing in the good emanating from Him according to their degree of perfection and remoteness from the center. Even the furthest removed from God parts of reality are not entirely empty of value. The assumption of the inherent goodness of the created world imparted to it by the Creator accompanied Christian thought, faithful on that point to the Book of Genesis, from its very beginning, championed, among others, by St. Augustine in his polemic against Manichaean dualism and Boethius.

Participation in a game requires that the player should "enter into a delicious speculation"; the value inherent in the world calls for a competent reader, who will be able to recognize and appreciate it. This does not mean that the goodness inherent in things is human subjective projection and depends for its reality on the human evaluating mind. Cusanus expressly addresses the possibility of a subjectivist interpretation of the world of values and rejects it in no uncertain terms. The true ontological ground of the reality of goods encountered in human experience is not human mind but the Absolute Value which exists objectively and does not depend for its reality on human perception and appreciation:

> For it is not the case that just because the mind sees that which is worth all things, it itself is worth all things. For values are not present in the mind as in their Essence but [are present there] as in a conception of them. For value is something real (just as the value of a mind is something existent and something real); and in that way value is

present in God as in [Him who is] the Essence of value. Value is also a conceptual being, because it can be known; and in that way it is present in the intellect as in a knower of value; it is not present there as in a greater value or as in the cause and essence of value. For it is not the case that just because our intellect knows a greater or a lesser value, it itself is a greater or a lesser value; for this knowledge [of value] does not give being to value.[17]

To make this point clear beyond all doubt, Cusanus draws an elaborate analogy between the way God-instituted values are perceived and made to operate in the God-made Universe and the way economic value carried by money is made to function in the familiar context of monetary economy involving production of money, that is, in Cusanus's time, minting coins and the minter, who is responsible for it; banking, that is evaluation of existing currencies; the banker, who performs this function; and, of course, the users. In the dialogue, it is Prince Albert who suggests this analogy:

It seems that if we liken God to a Minter of coins, the intellect will be like a banker. *Cardinal*: This is not an absurd likeness if you conceive of God as an Omnipotent Minter who can produce all coinage by means of His excellent and omnipotent power. To suppose the following would be a fitting likeness; Some [minter] is of such great power that by his own hand he produces whatever coinage he wills to. And he establishes a banker who has in his power the discernment of all the coins and a knowledge of counting—with the art of minting being reserved only for the minter. The banker makes known the coins' nobility, as well as [making known] the value, number, weight, and measure that the coinage has from [the minter, viz.,] God, so that the price of the minter's money and its value—and thereby the power of the minter—become known.[18]

God the Creator can indeed be regarded as the all-powerful Minter, whose sovereign power is to put into circulation whatever coins-things He finds suitable. The picture of God-the Supreme Minter captures well both His sovereign power and freedom and the inherent goodness and value of His creatures; it represents His creative activity as a wise and benevolent *oikonomia*. As Devin Singh observes, economic categories are useful for representing God's governance of the world:

The operations of money as a sign of power, representing authority and disciplining subjects accordingly, coincide with the financial trace in *oikonomia*. As such, these key functions of money became useful for the theological doctrines that emerged as thinkers considered and articulated the *oikonomia* of God as both a father and a king, ruling an *oikos* as well as a *polis*.[19]

In the image of God-the Supreme Minter drawn by Nicholas, it is emphasized that God is not only the producer of the coins-things but also the exemplar they imitate. The visage of the ruler impressed on a coin was a reminder of his sovereign power and the extent of his rule. But how can an image of God the Creator be impressed on a coin-thing, if Scripture assures us that *No one has ever seen God* (John 1, 18)? The image of the invisible God, the firstborn over all creation (Col 1:15), the exact representation of His being and the radiance of God's glory (Heb 1:3) and the appearance of His Essence (Heb 1:3), is the Son, so every coin-thing forged by the Supreme Minter bears His likeness impressed on it[20]:

That which makes [the material] to be coinage, or a coin, is the image, or sign, of him from whom it issues. But if it issues from the minter, then it bears his image, viz., the likeness of his face (...). Face is knowledge; by means of its face we distinguish one coin from another. Therefore, there is a single face of the minter; by means thereof he is known, and it reveals him who otherwise would be invisible and unknowable. And since the likeness of his face is present on all the coins, the likeness displays only a knowledge of— i.e., only the face of—the minter, from whom the coinage issues. Now, the image [on a coin] is nothing other than an inscribed name. Accordingly, Christ asked, "of whom is the coin's image and inscription?" They answered: "Of Caesar." Therefore, the Minter's Face and Name and the Figure-of-His-substance and His Son are the same thing. Therefore, the Son is the Father's Living Image and is the Figure of the Father's substance and is the Father's Splendor. Through the Son the Father-Minter makes, or mints, or places, His sign upon all things.[21]

Coins-things produced by the Minter-Creator and bearing His likeness impressed on them are so many points where the Divine transcendence and immanence meet, for a coin-thing is constituted in matter and must be multiplied if it is to serve as a currency. Yet the multiplicity of coins in no way impairs the unity of their exemplar but refers to it just as plurality of signs signifying one thing points to that very same thing:

Therefore, the Creator-Minter is present in all the coins by means of the Figure of His substance, just as a single signified thing is present in its many signs. For if, in all the coins, I behold the quiddity of that which is signified, I see only the one from whom the coinage issues.

But if I turn toward the signs that characterize the coins, I see the plurality of the coins, because the one signified-thing I see to be signified by means of many signs.[22]

A coin is constituted as a coin not by the material in which it has been forged but by the pattern and, above all, the image impressed by it, which also determines its value and the extent of its circulation. Cusanus further elucidates this image by reference to his own theory of diverse forms in which the divine transcendence and immanence appear and the dialectical relation between them. God, the infinite actuality (the aspect of His transcendence), impresses His Image in matter and puts thus informed piece into circulation in order to multiply His presence in the created domain which is His work (in which consists His immanence):

> But notice that when what is mintable is imprinted with a sign, it is a coin or is coinage. For example, imprinted copper—imprinted, that is, with a sign of the likeness of the imprinter—is coinage. Mintable material becomes a coin by means of the sign. And it is called 'imprinted material, or befigured material, that has received a determination of its possibility-of-being-a-coin.' In this way, I see the signified (1) prior to its sign, (2) in its sign, and (3) subsequently to its sign: prior to its sign [I see it] as the true nature (veritas) that precedes its own befigurement; in its sign [I see it] as the true nature in its own image; and subsequently to its sign [I see it] as what-is-signified is signified by its sign.[23]

But if every coin-thing put in circulation bears the imprint of the Son, this metaphor of the divine monetary economy serves to represent not only the work of Creation but also the work of Redemption as well. The supreme realization of the divine *oikonomia* with respect to the world took place, thanks to the Coin which was the person of Jesus Christ, who was the price paid for the redemption of mankind from the slavery of sin. The divine currency which was Jesus Christ, once put in circulation, enlarges the dominion of God and lies foundation for a new kind of divine economy: the economy of grace.[24]

This economic and monetary symbolism, already well established in the patristic thought, as Devin Singh and Giorgio Agamben have shown, was taken up by Cusanus in the new context of the dynamic economic development that Europe experienced halfway through the 15th century. As Singh observes, the use of monetary metaphors was widespread in the patristic context:

> The language of money, currency, and coinage is employed in patristic thought both to depict human nature and salvation and to describe Christ and his work. Humans are portrayed as coins, impressed with

the image of their creator. This image has been eroded by sin but is renewed by a fresh stamping or reminting by the savior. Christ is the paradigmatic image, the stamp used to make impressions of the *imago Dei* on humanity. He is thus incarnated as the chief coin, as the governing materialization of this ideal monetary image. Soteriological language of reminting and reissuing coins coincides with the widespread ancient practice of monarchs declaring their reign through new coin types. The fresh reminting of humanity thus proclaims the inbreaking kingdom of God.[25]

Nicholas assimilated this language of monetary symbolism and ingeniously used it to elucidate his own system of thought, adding to the inherited array of symbolic representations new aspects and contexts of reference. His own contribution to the language of economic theology seems to the emphasis put on the role and importance of the banker: a coin issued by the Minter and bearing His imprint must be received by the banker, who alone can recognize and appreciate it and then put it in circulation, for it to serve as an accepted currency. Since the function of recognition and appreciation is fulfilled by intellect, it is intellect that is the banker in the world of divine *oikonomia* and the divine monetary policy. Thus, the role of the banker-the intellect is indispensable, yet, interestingly, the banker himself is a coin, and in some other context is referred to as one. Since the image impressed on divinely instituted coins is that of God, the Son, even God, the supreme Minter can be referred to as a coin. Therefore, Cusanus states: "Therefore, the intellect is that coin which is also a banker, even as God is that coin which is also a Minter."[26]

Thus, the central place in Cusanus's thought belongs to man: man is both a coin and a banker, and it is because of man and for man that the divine *oikonomia* works, both as the work of creation and that of redemption.

Notes

1 LG II, 110, p. 1242.
2 LG II, 111, p. 1242.
3 Cf. MARCIN BUKAŁA. "Scholastic Concepts Concerning the Idea of Economic Value." in: *I Beni di questo mondo. Teorie etico-economiche nel laboratorio dell'Europa medieval,* eds. R. Lambertini, L. Sileo, Fédération Internationale des Instituts d'Etudes Médiévales, Porto, 2010, pp. 351–352.
4 Cf. BOETHIUS. "How substances can be good in virtue of their existence without being absolute goods." in: *The Theological Tractates,* trans. by H. F. Stewart, E. K. Rand, Heinemann, London, Harvard University Press, Cambridge, MA, 1968, pp. 42–43.
5 Cf. IAN A. AERTSEN. *Medieval Philosophy and the Transcendentals. The Case of Thomas Aquinas,* Brill, Leiden-New York-Köln, 1996, pp. 17–24. Cusanus owned and read several Aquinas's works. Cf. MARKUS FÜHRER.

Echoes of Aquinas in Cusanus's Vision of Man, Lexington Books, Lanham-Boulder-New York-Toronto-Plymouth, 2014 (e-book).

6 ROMAN INGARDEN. *Man and Value*, trans. by A. Szylewicz, Philosophia Verlag, München-Wien, The Catholic University of America Press, Washington D. C., 1983, pp. 143–144.

7 Cf. CLYDE L. MILLER. *Reading Cusanus*. Metaphor and Dialectic in a Conjectural Universe, The Catholic University of America Press, Washington D.C., 2003, pp. 137–138, footnote 44.

8 Cf. DM III, 69, p. 542. Cf. AGNIESZKA KIJEWSKA. "Idiota de mente: Cusanus' Position in the Debate between Aristotelianism and Platonism," in: *Nicholas of Cusa on the Self and Self-Consciousness*, eds. W. A. Euler, Y. Gustafsson, I. Wikström, Abo Akademi University Press, Abo, 2010, pp. 84–86.

9 Cf. TONI RONNOW-RASMUSSEN. "Intrinsic an Extrinsic Value," in: *The Oxford Handbook of Value Theory*, ed. by I. Hirose, J. Olson, Oxford University Press, Oxford, 2015, p. 29: "The concept of intrinsic value has been glossed variously as what is *valuable for its own sake, in itself, on its own right*, as *an end*, or *as such*. By contrast, extrinsic value has been characterized mainly as what is valuable as a means, or for something else's sake."

10 SINGH. *Divine Currency*. The Theological Power of Money in the West, Stanford University Press, Stanford, CA, 2018, pp. 5–6.

11 There, p. 6.

12 Cf. there, p. 36.

13 LG II, 64, pp. 1214–1215.

14 There is a typical Neoplatonic tenet in Cusanus's system and he could succeed it to Eriugena. Cf. STEPHEN GERSH. "Omnipresence in Eriugena. Some Reflections on Augustino-Maximian Element in 'Periphyseon'," in: *Eriugena. Studien zu seinen Quellen, Vorträge des II. Internationalen Eriugena-Colloquiums*, ed. by W. Beierwaltes, Carl Winter Universitätsverlag, Heidelberg, 1980, pp. 55–57.

15 LG II, 107, pp. 1239–1240.

16 LG II, 110, p. 1242.

17 LG II, 112, p. 1243.

18 LG II, 115, p. 1244.

19 SINGH. *Divine Currency*, pp. 104–105.

20 Cf. MARIE-JOSE MONDZAIN. *Image, Icon, Economy. The Byzantine Origins of the Contemporary Imaginary*, trans. by R. Franses, Stanford University Press, Stanford, CA, 2005, pp. 69–117 (Chapter 3: *The Doctrine of the Image and Icon*).

21 LG II, 116–117, p. 1245.

22 LG II, 117, p. 1245.

23 LG II, 118, p. 1246.

24 Cf. KATHRYN TANNER. *Economy of Grace*, Fortress Press, Minneapolis, 2005, p. 6: "The history of Christian faith and practice is full of the search for signs of grace, money being just one of them."

25 SINGH. *Divine Currency*, p.105.

26 LG II, 119, p. 1247.

8 The circle of rational player and efficient banker

Among the qualities that should characterize a participant in a game of contest, named as one of the most indispensable, was ability to use his/her reason, that is to conduct himself/herself in a rational and purposeful way. Ability to act in a rational way and perform various operations requiring use of reason, such as calculating, planning, evaluating, inventing strategies, etc., is certainly required of a good bank manager. What is undoubtedly true for a competitor in a game and a banker is by far more so for a participant in the supreme game, the game of life. Thus, every human being is called upon to live by his/her reason and presumably endowed with all necessary prerequisites for doing so. Let us consider what Nicholas of Cusa thought of rationality as the most essential quality of man and what place he assigned to reason in the structure of man as a being.

In accordance with this opinion, it can perhaps be conceded that the world is threefold: a small world that is man, a maximal world that is God and a large world that is called Universe. The small world is a likeness of the large world; the large world is a likeness of the maximal world. But at the end of the first book of *The Bowling-Game*, Prince John makes the following observation: "since man is a small world, I have doubts about whether he is a part of the large world."[1] This remark introduces an old and much explored in the past Platonic theme of the essential analogy obtaining between the structure of the Universe as a whole and the structure of man as a being; on the basis of that analogy, man is described as a "small cosmos" or "small world" or simply, a microcosm. Cusanus was well aware of the significance of this topic and introduced the term and the concept of man as microcosm in his first, strictly philosophico-theological treatise *On Leraned Ignorance*.[2]

A comprehensive account of the history of the medieval discussions of that topic was presented by Marian Kurdziałek in his article *Mediaeval Doctrines on Man as Image of the World*. According to him, the conception of man as microcosm had been rooted in the teaching of Plato and his synthetic, organic vision of man and human society as orderly structures, modelled on the cosmic order and structure of the Universe.

DOI: 10.4324/9781003310693-8

An individual human being was viewed as a reduced copy of the cosmos, containing all the component elements thereof structured basically in the same way as in the Universe. Some Christian thinkers in late antiquity and the Middle Ages took up this Platonic conception prompted by a certain interpretation of Mark 16: 15: "preach the gospel to all creation," "all creation" being taken to mean man. Seen as "all creation," man was thought to be equal in dignity to the whole Universe and to be a faithful likeness of it both in his composition of elementary constituents and in his essential structure. The likeness obtaining between man and the Universe could be seen as concerning mainly the structure of the body (the Platonic-Pythagorean cosmological interpretation), the structure of man's inner being or soul (the psychological interpretation), the aspect of the human psycho-physical unity (the Platonic structural ontological interpretation), as well as the forms of social and political life created by man (Platonic social-political interpretation). Kurdziałek presents a detailed account of that microcosmic theory of man as developed mainly in the neoplatonic context:

> In the light of the above doctrines there took shape the following doctrine of man as an image of the world, as a microcosm: the human soul, together with its ethereal and luminous body, constitutes the genus of the "internal man" ("homo caelestis"), of a microcosm *kat'egzochen*, since the ether as the most perfect of the elements unites in itself the natures of the elements of the meteorological region; the body created out of these elements would be merely an external manifestation, a terrestrial annex ("homo mundanus"), a microcosm which could be comprehended with the senses. The conviction nursed by the pagan and Christian neo-Platonists, that in the human phenomenon there appear both all the powers of the soul (divine—"intelligentia," human—"ratio," animal—"sensus," vegetable—"vita"), and all kinds of elements and bodies, resulted in man's being set in opposition to them as a "magnum miraculum [...] animal adorandum atque honorandum [...] feliciore loco medietatis positus," "omnium officina," "omnium conclusio," "medietas atque adunatio," "nexus," "nodus," "vinculum," "catena," "clausula," "horizon."[3]

The descriptions of man quoted here have been taken mostly from *Asclepius*, a Hermetic treatise, and from the works of Eriugena and Honorius Augustodunensis, all of which were familiar to Nicholas of Cusa, who drew from them his knowledge of the microcosmic tradition.[4] In point of fact, all the characteristic themes of microcosmic anthropology as distinguished by Kurdziałek can be found in Cusanus's thought, where they serve as means of highlighting the exceptional position of man in the work of creation. Cusanus's anthropological concerns were of a piece with the general spirit of his time, marked by the ascent of humanism and producing speeches and essays in praise of human dignity and greatness.[5] The theme of human greatness appears also in *The Bowling-Game:* to Prince John's doubts concerning whether man should be regarded as a world in its own right or as a part of the large world, the Cardinal responds as follows:

> Assuredly, man is a small world in such a way that he is also a part of the large world. Now, a whole shines forth in all its parts, since a part is a part of the whole. Just as the whole man shines forth in the hand, which is proportioned to the whole, but, nevertheless, the whole perfection of man shines forth in a more perfect manner in the head: so the universe shines forth in each of its parts, for all things have their respective relation and proportion to the universe, but, nevertheless, the universe shines forth more greatly in that part which is called man than in any other part. Therefore, because the perfection of the totality of the universe shines forth more greatly in and through man, man is a perfect, but small, world and is a part of the large world.[6]

With this statement, the conversation embarks upon further exploration of man's metaphysical constitution, his relationship with the Universe at large and, most importantly, his autonomy and sovereignty over the small domain of his own affairs. Through his body, man is part of the Universe and subject to the kingdom of the world; however, with the imposition of the intellectual soul, which is created immediately by God, he becomes king in his own right. It is the intellectual soul that makes him an autonomous ruler in his own kingdom:

> *John*: If I understand rightly, then just as the universe is one large kingdom, so also man is a kingdom (but a small one) in a large kingdom, just as the kingdom of Bohemia is present in the kingdom of the Romans, i.e., in the universal empire. *Cardinal*: Excellent! For man is a kingdom similar to the kingdom of the universe: [he is a kingdom] grounded in a part of the universe. For example, when he is an embryo in his mother's womb, his own kingdom does not yet exist. But after the creation of the intellectual soul, which is imposed by an act of creation, there arises a kingdom having its own king, and it is called a man. When the soul departs, he stops being a man and a kingdom.[7]

The human body with its sense apparatus has been created for the soul, to minister to the soul's needs.[8] The soul is the substantial principle which unifies and organizes the human body. This principle Cusanus refers to, depending on the context, as the mind (*mens*) or as the soul (*anima*), that is the principle of life. When thought of as the source of life for its body, it is appropriately called soul, when considered as judging and naming all things in its invisible depth, it is rightly referred to as mind. It is above all the human soul in its function of the mind that is most properly described as a microcosm, for it intentionally contains in itself in a contracted way the whole of created reality. The mind is the substantial form of a human entity, which "enfolds" in itself all other faculties and powers exercised by the soul, including vegetative and sense powers and reason and intellect, and the lower faculties exist in a more perfect way in the mind than in themselves, that is in an "unfolded" form.[9] In his first work, *On Learned Ignorance,* Nicholas named three cognitive faculties in human beings: senses, intellect and reason.[10] The same list of human faculties is given in *On Surmises,* and in *Layman on Mind,* where the background for the discussion provides the Boethian-Chartrian methodology, which, having assumed the triple division of speculative philosophy into physics, mathematics and theology assigned to each science its own *modus procedendi* according to the nature of its subject and the triple hierarchy of human cognitive faculties.[11] Drawing on the fund of ideas handed down in the Boethian tradition, Cusanus's theory of knowledge broke with the dominant in Scholasticism conception of cognition as a passive and receptive process (the passivity and receptivity was thought to ensure realism of knowledge), determined entirely by the object, and replaced it with a conception that attributed some active role in the process of acquiring knowledge to cognitive faculties. The cognitive faculty is not a passive receiver in the process of cognition; on the contrary, it is operative and actively contributes to the outcome of the process. The principal active function of cognitive faculties lies in discernment and the judgment based on it. According to Nicholas, the process of acquisition of knowledge consists both in the assimilation of the knower to the known object (the passive side of the process) and in measuring the cognized object (the active aspect of a cognitive act); the latter function is so important that even the Latin name for mind – *mens* – is derived from it.[12]

> Mind is so assimilative that in the sense of sight it assimilates itself to things visible, in the sense of hearing it assimilates itself to things audible, in the sense of taste to things tasteable, in the sense of smell to things that can be smelled, in the sense of touch to things touchable. In the senses [mind assimilates itself] to things perceptible, in the imagination to things imaginable, and in reason to things accessible

by reasoning. For example, imagination, in the absence of perceptible things, is like a sense that is without the power to discriminate between perceptible things. (...) But in association with reason imagination conforms itself to things, while discriminating one state from another. In all these instances our mind operates in the spirit of the arteries. When our mind is stimulated by encountering the forms conveyed, in a replicated way, from the objects unto the spirit [of the arteries]: by means of [these perceptual] forms our mind assimilates itself to the objects, so that by way of the assimilation it makes a judgment regarding the object. Hence, that subtle spirit-of-the-arteries, which is enlivened by mind, is fashioned by mind into a likeness of the [perceptual] form, which has presented [itself as] an obstacle to [this] spirit's motion.[13]

In his discussion of the process of acquisition of knowledge, Cusanus does not forget the mechanism of sense perception and produces a fairly sophisticated account of it. The key notion in this account is that of vital spirits; very subtle material particles, which emanate from the sense organs and by encountering the objects of sense perception, are reflected back carrying with themselves the form of the encountered object. The mind, encountering these forms conveyed to the spirit of the arteries, receives a stimulus and in accordance with these forms assimilates itself to the encountered objects of perception.[14] The vital spirits, capable of a sort of interaction with material objects of sense perception as well as with the mind, function as an intermediary and a meeting point between the material world of bodies and the real of spirit.[15]

The vegetative and sensible faculties of man bind him to the surrounding corporeal world, which is changeable and transient. For sense perception to get fixed and stabilized and somehow preserved in time, what is needed is the intervention of reason (Platonic *dianoia*), which alone can render to sense perception its meaningful place and function in human life. The role of the intermediary between senses and reason fulfils imagination which brings together and synthesizes contributions of all the senses. Yet both the external senses and imagination are subordinated to reason, whose pre-eminence consists in its power to introduce order into the multiplicity of data delivered by the sense faculties and to pass judgment about them, thus discerning between various sorts of them and classifying them according to various categories. The judgment of reason is given always in the light of the principle of non-contradiction; therefore, reason becomes helpless when faced with paradox.[16]

Besides its all-important theoretical functions, reason fulfils an absolutely fundamental role in the sphere of practical life: it is its job in this domain to direct human conduct, and in particular its function is to master and control the irrational passions and desires in human beings.

When properly fulfilling its task, reason "tempers and calms the passions, in order that a human being will not make a goal of perceptible things and be deprived of his intellect's spiritual desire."[17] This shows clearly that reason fulfils the mediating function in the complete structure of all human faculties.

Yet even reason, for all its importance, is not the most essential and the most elevated power with which human being has been endowed. That highest faculty, in which all other faculties are enfolded, is intellect, sometimes referred to, following the example of the masters of Chartres, as intelligence. It is only thanks to intellect, that man can be called a kingdom in its own right, independent and autonomous, and ruled by its own king. Not only is this faculty the source of the perfection and autonomy of man as a being, for it is also in this sphere of human person that the greatest similitude of man to God resides:

> For a man is his own intellect. In the intellect the perceptual contractedness is somehow subsumed in (*suppositatur*) the intellectual nature, which exists as a certain divine, separate, abstract being, while the perceptual remains temporal and corruptible in accordance with its own nature.[18]

Cusanus's conception of intellect is firmly rooted in the philosophical tradition originating with Plato, in Plato's conception of *nous* and its proper function, which is the direct insight into the eternal, immutable, intelligible reality of transcendent Forms. For Nicholas of Cusa, intellect, like Plato's *nous*, is the power of direct, non-sensible, intuitive cognition whose cognitive activity is often likened to seeing. When referring to intellectual vision, Cusanus used the metaphor of "the mind's eye," familiar to philosophers, starting with Plato, through Neoplatonists, Chaldean Oracles ("the flower of intellect"), up to Boethius:

> But the mind's eye, which looks unto intelligible things, which are above the imagination, cannot deny that it (1) sees the fact that all things—including imagination—are contained in being, which is beyond imagination, and (2) sees that unless being were in the things contained [by it], this [first] fact would not be true.[19]

The relevant passages in *The Vision of God* are even more telling, but the quoted statement is enough to let us grasp the most salient features of intellectual cognition, which is a kind of vision: (1) The act of intellectual vision is constituted by being directed to an object; it is an act of intellectually seeing an object, which means that it is characterized by intentionality essential to every true cognitive ("…looks unto intelligible things"). (2) The object of intellectual vision is grasped in its entirety, at once, that is in an instant, and immediately. This object co-determines the nature of that act of intellectual vision ("...cannot deny that ... all things"). (3) The mind's eye grasps its object as existing ("...all things ... are contained in being"): it cannot be directed to something that does not exist, as the intellectual vision unveils the truth (4) of the given thing's being. And if every thing is in its own way a manifestation of God, God is the Exemplar and the Truth of every single creature. The truth of the intellectual vision is understood not in the sense of the classical definition in terms of adequation of thing with the intellect but rather as "unveiling" (Heidegger's *altheia*) of the relation of things to their Divine source. This special understanding of truth inherent in acts of intellectual vision may well constitute a special "quality" of that kind of cognitive acts.[20] In consequence, that truth-orientation of acts of intellectual vision reveals that which turns out to be a necessary a priori condition of such acts taking place, namely a certain notion of God inscribed in human mind. I will come back to this point and explore it from a slightly different perspective.

This survey of the most characteristic features of Cusanus's conception of intellect and intellectual vision makes it clear why he attributes to that faculty the pride of place in the structure of human being over all the other faculties. The human intellect dwells in man like a sovereign in his kingdom, whose presence invests the kingdom with independence and autonomy. The hierarchical order of the faculties informing human essence, rising from the humblest material and vegetative level to the lofty level of intellectual vision, which opens the way to communing with God, inspired the philosopher of Cusa with admiration for God's work of creation. In *On Surmises*, he gave expression to this feeling by inserting in this treatise a passage, which, while being a eulogy of man, amounts to the highest praise of the Author of the wonderful work of human essence:

> Marvelous is this work of God in which the discriminating power is conducted, progressively, from the center of the senses upwards unto the very lofty intellectual nature! It is conducted by means of certain gradations and certain instrumental channels in which its ties with the very refined corporeal spirit are continuously made clearer and more simplified, on account of the triumph of the soul's power; [these ties are lucidified and simplified] until they arrive at the repository of rational power. Afterwards, [the discriminating power] arrives at the very lofty order of intellectual power (as if arriving at the boundless sea by means of a stream), where there are surmised to be choirs of learning, of intelligence, and of most simple intellectuality.[21]

Human intellectual vision, for all its sublimity, is still infinitely re-moved from the perfection of God's vision, in which all things are seen in one simple act, for it is the same for God to see and to create.[22] Cusa-nus believed that the Greek word *theos*, god, was derived from the verb *theoro*, I see. While God's seeing is the same thing as creating, that is instituting things in being: human vision (*theoria*), unable to cause any-thing to exist on its own (as distinct from existing merely as an idea in somebody's mind), imitates God's creative action by establishing a con-jectural world.[23]

Human mind is only an image of God's all-enfolding simplicity. God's knowledge is precise, leaving no objective content beyond its compre-hension, and certain, while human comprehension is always incomplete because always grasping its object from a certain limited perspective, one of many possible perspectives, and always leaving some objective content in the cognized thing beyond its grasp, which can always be made more complete. To illustrate this claim, Nicholas in his work *On Learned Ignorance* drew a famous comparison of human ever-increasing cognitions of a given thing to a series of ever greater polygons inscribed in a circle:

> Hence, the intellect, which is not truth, never comprehends truth so precisely that truth cannot be comprehended infinitely more pre-cisely. For the intellect is to truth as [an inscribed] polygon is to [the inscribing] circle. The more angles the inscribed polygon has the more similar it is to the circle. However, even if the number of its angles is increased ad infinitum, the polygon never becomes equal [to the circle] unless it is resolved into an identity with the circle. Hence, regarding truth, it is evident that we do not know anything other than the following: viz., that we know truth not to be precisely comprehensible as it is.[24]

If this may sound discouraging, Cusanus is far from being discour-aged: although we know we will never achieve precise knowledge of real things as they are in themselves, yet we can always get closer to it by ever renewing our efforts.

The process of progressive deepening of human knowledge and the mechanism of sense cognition came again under examination in the dia-logue *Layman on mind*. In that dialogue, Cusanus, in the words of the Layman, rejected *expressis verbis* the theory of innate ideas. According to the Layman, God united human mind to the body on purpose, in order that it may perfect itself through constant cognitive effort with the help of the body, and if man had his ideas implanted in him prior to any experience, he could realize his capacity for knowledge without any help from the body and the senses, which would then become superfluous.

And yet, just as the eye is made to see by receiving a stimulus from an external object, the mind begins to comprehend and form its concepts only when sensible things incite it into action through sense impressions.[25] The mind, when receiving stimuli from the senses, takes on the likeness of, or assimilates to, the provided sense data through the intermediary agency of vital spirits. However, this assimilation to sense data does not mean that the mind comes into possession of perfect or precise truth: the forms to which human mind can assimilate in the process of ordinary cognition based on sense experience are only secondary forms, the ones constituted in matter, which are merely images of pure forms, the exemplars and perfect measures in the process of cognitive discernment, which are constituted in the simplicity of Divine Mind. Thus, when human mind takes in the forms given in the sense experience, it merely approaches and never achieves the precise truth; the knowledge gained in human cognitive efforts remains ever conjectural knowledge or a surmise: it is always placed halfway along the way to the perfection of absolute truth, and it can always be made more precise, for example by taking into account new data and by adopting new points of view. To say this does not mean claiming that human knowledge is false; it only means that in their ordinary cognition, human beings can only achieve absolute truth "by means of otherness":

> Accordingly, it follows that every human affirmation about what is true is a surmise. For the increase in our apprehension of what is true is endless. Hence, since without [the aid of] any comparative relation our actual [increase] is directed toward this maximal, humanly unattainable knowledge, our weak apprehension's uncertain falling short of the pure truth implies that our affirmations about the true are surmises. Therefore, the unattainable oneness-of-truth is known by means of a surmising otherness; and the surmising otherness is known in and through a most simple oneness-of-truth. Hereafter, we will come to understand this matter more clearly.[26]

This conjectural or "surmising" nature characterizes both human ordinary everyday cognition and the strictly scientific one. As Tamara Albertini observed, "one's knowledge of nature too is essentially only 'conjectural.' Although it may partake of truth, a positively formulated scientific statement remains a matter of approximation, to be precise, of infinitesimal approximation." Thus, it can be said that Nicholas of Cusa appreciates "a scientific value of approximate data" and in this way anticipates modern scientific approach to empirical research.[27]

There is, however, a privileged domain, in which human knowledge is not a surmise but a precise grasp of the truth of the object as it is in itself. This exceptional domain is that of mathematics. Here the mind assimilates to numbers and figures as they are in themselves and not as they exist in a projection into matter. With these numbers and figures, the mind measures the things and passes judgment on them. The human measuring activity with respect to things deciphers and unveils God's design hidden in created things since, as Scripture assures us, God created "all things in number, weight, and measure, arranged the elements in an admirable order. (Number pertains to arithmetic, weight to music, measure to geometry.)"[28] The Divine Artificer in constructing the Universe made use of a whole array of means which are studied by the arts of *quadrivium* and which have been made available to man as a help in his exploration of the structure of created reality. And yet, how effective these human efforts in recovering God's hidden design in the world can be? Are human beings in a position to raise their understanding, even with the help of the means provided by mathematics, to the level of a comprehension of God? If cognition consists essentially in numbering and measuring, obviously there will be no proportion and no contact between the final human efforts and the infinity of God's designs.[29]

Yet, despite this massive disproportion, some perception of divine reality is available to human mind, according to Cusanus. Mathematical studies, and in particular interpreting the symbolism of mathematical notion, provides some preparation for intellectual perception of divine reality. Involved in these preparatory studies will be the faculty of reason, whose involvement, however, fulfils only a propaedeutical function: the efforts in interpreting the meaning of mathematical symbols opens the way for the activity of intellect, which in this way will be raised to the level where it can gain insight into the reality of God. The method of preparing the way for the contemplation of God by studying mathematical figures was characteristic of Cusanus and could be described as the "way of theological figures." The starting point for this method is attending some properties of geometrical figures, which at first are considered in terms of their finite geometrical properties. The next step consists in extending in thought these figure or some parts of them to infinity. When this is done, it will become evident to the contemplating mind that in infinity all different figures coincide and become one: a triangle, a circle, a sphere when extended to infinity become indistinguishable from an infinite line. This enables the intellect to grasp how contraries and differences resolve into unity when raised to infinity. The last step in this consideration consists in carrying over this property of geometrical infinity onto Infinite God and realizing that in Him this resolution of opposites becomes true in the highest degree and contradictions resolve into a higher unity.[30]

This exercise in rising from simple mathematical speculation up to an insight into the nature of the Absolute Being would never be attempted if the man who undertakes it did not have an experience of foretasting (*praegustare*) that sort of intellectual contemplation. This foretaste awakens in man the desire for intellectual comprehension:

> This movement is a proceeding—by means of understanding— unto its own object, which is Absolute Truth, which itself is Eternal Wisdom. Now, since that proceeding is understanding, it is also intellectually tasting. For to apprehend with the intellect is to attain—in the best way possible and by means of a most pleasant tasting—unto quiddity. For through a sensible tasting, which does not pertain to the quiddity of a thing, we perceive—by means of the sense [of taste]—a pleasing deliciousness in [the properties] external to the quiddity. In a similar way, we taste—by means of the intellect and with regard to the quiddity—an intellectual delightfulness, which is the image of the delightfulness of Eternal Wisdom, the Quiddity of quiddities.[31]

And yet, the intellect cannot get a 'foretaste' of God merely by experiencing and comprehending finite things, so there must be some other way of getting a glimpse of Divine Reality even before one is properly educated to undertake the contemplation thereof. This glimpse and foretaste is provided by the fact that human mind is indeed endowed with a primitive and undeveloped notion of God. This is shown by the fact that we spontaneously know what it means to cognize and to measure. But measuring presupposes a primary unit with which to measure all things; consequently, we must have a notion of a primary measure. It turns out that this notion of primary and absolute measure is no other than the primitive and unclear notion of God, for God indeed is the Absolute Measure that the Presupposition of all things in general and each and every thing in particular. Thus, this primary notion of God is a priori present in the human mind and is a necessary condition for the functioning of the mind, for forming other concepts and for the use of the language. This a priori concept of God present in every human mind is the "concept of concepts," as the Layman says in the dialogue On Wisdom:

> *Orator*: [I want you] to tell me how I am to form a concept of God, since He is greater than can be conceived. *Layman*: [You may do so] just as [you form a concept] of concept. (...) You have heard how it is that in every conceiving the Inconceivable is conceived. Therefore, the concept of concept approaches the Inconceivable. *Orator*: How, then, may I form a more precise concept [of God].[32]

The "concept of concepts" turns out to be the first and necessary condition for acquiring any conceptual knowledge; it is inscribed in our minds and the absolute presupposition for all their operations. This does not mean, however, that immediately become aware of its presence in our minds; on the contrary, it takes a long and arduous process of reflection on the structure and working of our cognitive activity, and in particular on the failures and limitations of it. In order to discover this concept in ourselves, we should take a look into the depths of our minds or to employ "the mind's eye":

> Therefore, if someone looks, with profundity of mind, unto the simplicity of Absolute Reason, which antecedently enfolds within itself all things, he makes a concept of the Concept-per-se, i.e., of the Absolute Concept.[33]

The notion of God as the "first thing known" (*primum cognitum*), which is the a priori necessary condition for man acquiring any knowledge, was known to Cusanus from his study of Scholastic writers: St. Bonaventure or Duns Scotus. He also quoted some books of the Bible in support of his conception, for example *Wisdom dwells in the highest* (Ecl. 24:4) and *Wisdom proclaims [itself] openly in the streets* (Prov 1:20).[34]

To come back to our concern with the game and what it can teach us about the most weight concerns of our life, Cusanus believes that essential points of his conception of human knowledge, its preconditions, structure, development and the ultimate end can be confirmed by considering some aspects of this organized social entertainment which is playing at a game with fixed rules. Also managing finances involves the activity of the mind and is essentially a purpose-oriented activity. Both participation in a game and management of monetary resources can offer interesting analogies, which may help us better to understand and fulfil our lives' central task. Both the player and the banker seek some sort of fulfilment and use their resources, and in particular, their acumen and skill and the already acquired knowledge, to that purpose, in which they both come as an illustration of that game, in which all of us are necessarily involved: the game of human life. Since we all seek fulfilment, we will all meet in the last circle of the bowling game: the circle of fulfilment. There we will also meet the player, the banker and the philosopher, who follows and interprets the actions and dispositions of both and offers us his guidance and advice along our own way to fulfilment. The philosopher, who evaluates the goods in the light of intellect, perhaps the most, deserves to be described as the banker of intellectual goods and, perhaps to him, as a representative of intellect, can be referred the following words: "Therefore, the intellect is that coin which is also a banker, even as God is that coin which is also a Minter."[35]

Notes

1 LG I, 42, p. 1201.
2 DI III, 198, p. 119.
3 MARIAN KURDZIAŁEK. "Mediaeval Doctrines of Man as Image of the World." *Roczniki Filozoficzne*, 62, n. 4, 2014, pp. 213–214; cf. PAULINE M. WATTS. "Renaissance Humanism," in: *Introducing Nicholas of Cusa. A Guide to a Renaissance Man*, eds. Ch. M. Bellito, Th. M. Izbicki, G. Christianson, Paulist Press, New York-Mahwah, NJ, 2004, pp. 178–179.
4 Nicholas of Cusa annotated the first book of Eriugena's *Periphyseon*. Cf. DONALD F. DUCLOW. "Coinciding in the Margins: Cusanus glosses Eriugena," in: *Eriugena-Cusanus*, eds. A. Kijewska, R. Majeran, H. Schwaetzer, Wydawnictwo KUL, Lublin, 2011, pp. 83–103.
5 Cf. WATTS. "Renaissance Humanism," pp. 172–173.
6 LG I, 42, p. 1202.
7 LG I, 43, p. 1202.
8 Cf. DC II, 10, 121, p. 225.
9 Cf. DM V, 80, p. 547.
10 DI III, 6, 215, p. 127.
11 AGNIESZKA KIJEWSKA. "Mathematics as a Preparation for Theology: Boethius, Eriugena, Thierry of Chartres," in: *Boèce ou la chaine du savoirs*, ed. A. Galonnier, Peeters, Louvain-Paris, 2003, pp. 633–637.
12 DM, I, 57, p. 536. Cf. CLYDE L. MILLER. *Reading Cusanus*. Metaphor and Dialectic in a Conjectural Universe, The Catholic University of America Press, Washington, D.C., 2003, pp. 127–146.
13 DM VII, 100, p. 557.
14 Cf. AGNIESZKA KIJEWSKA. "Idiota de mente: Cusanus' Position in the Debate between Aristotelianism and Platonism." in: Nicholas of Cusa on the Self and Self-Consciousness, eds. W. A. Euler, Y. Gustafsson, I. Wikström, Abo Akademi University Press, Abo, 2010, pp. 81–82.
15 DM VIII, 112–113, p. 563.
16 Cf. JEAN-MARIE NICOLLE. "Quelques sources philosophico-mathématiques de Nicolas de Cues," in: *Nicolas de Cues, les méthodes d'une pensées*, ed. J.-M. Counet, S. Mercier, Institute de L'Etudes Médiévales, Louvain-la-Neuve, 2005, p. 48.
17 DI III, 6, 215, p. 127.
18 DI III, 4, p. 123.
19 LG II, 67, p. 1216. Cf. Plato, *The Republic* 533 C-D, trans. by G. M. A. Grube, Hackett Publishing Company, Indianapolis, 1974, pp. 184–185; BOECE. *Institution Arithmétique* I, I, 7, ed. J.-Y. Gillaumin, Les Belles Lettres, Paris, 1995, p. 8.
20 Cf. VD VII, 25, p. 691; Cf. AGNIESZKA KIJEWSKA. "*Infinitatem te video*. La conception de l'Infinité de Dieu dans le traité *L'Icône ou la vision de Dieu*," in : *Infini et altérité dans l'oeuvre de Nicolas de Cues (1401-1464)*, ed. H. Pasqua, Louvain-la-Neuve, Peeters, 2017, pp. 195–196.
21 DC II, 13, 142, p. 236.
22 CLYDE L. MILLER. "Knowledge and Human Mind," in: *Introducing Nicholas of Cusa. A Guide to a Renaissance Man*, eds. Ch. M. Bellito, Th. M. Izbicki, G. Christianson, Paulist Press, New York-Mahwah, NJ, 2004, pp. 301–302. VD 10, 41, p. 698; There, 12, 48, p. 702: "For Your seeing gives being, because [Your seeing] is Your essence."
23 VD V, 18, p. 687; Cf. AGNIESZKA KIJEWSKA. "Etymology and Philosophy: God as Videns and Currens," in: *Eriugena-Cusanus*, eds. A. Kijewska, R. Majeran, H. Schwaetzer, Wydawnictwo KUL, Lublin, 2011, pp. 124–126.

24 DI I, 3, 10, p. 8. Cf. CLYDE L. MILLER. *The Art of Conjecture. Nicholas of Cusa on Knowledge*, Catholic University of America Press, Washington, D. C., 2021, pp. 13–22.

25 Cf. DM IV, 77, pp. 545–546. Nevertheless, Cusanus does not propose the theory of abstraction as the method of construction of the concepts. Cf. JEAN-MICHEL COUNET. *Mathématiques et dialectiques chez Nicolas de Cues*, Librairie Vrin, Paris, 2000, p. 301.

26 DC, prol. 2, p. 163; cf. MILLER. "Knowledge and Human Mind," pp. 303–304.

27 TAMARA ALBERTINI. "Mathematics and Astronomy," in: *Introducing Nicholas of Cusa. A Guide to a Renaissance Man*, eds. Ch. M. Bellito, Th. M. Izbicki, G. Christianson, Paulist Press, New York-Mahwah, NJ, 2004, pp. 374–375.

28 DI II, 13, 176, p. 99.

29 Cf. DI I, 3, 9, p. 7. Cf. AGNIESZKA KIJEWSKA. "Conception of Intellect in Eriugena and Cusanus," in: *Nicolaus Cusanus: ein bewundernswerter historischer Brennpunkt*, eds. K. Reinhardt, H. Schwaetzer, Roderer-Verlag, Regensburg, 2008, pp. 18–19.

30 Cf. DI I, 13, 33, p. 20.

31 DS I, 26, p. 510.

32 DS II, 28, p. 511.

33 DS II, 35, p. 514.

34 DS I, 7, p. 500; I, 8, p. 501; I, 10, p. 502; I, 20, p. 507; I, 3–5, p. 498.

35 LG II, 119, p. 1247.

9 The last circle of the game of bowls and the game of human life

The circle of fulfilment

The ball used in the bowling game and the movements it performs in the course of it can be interpreted as symbols of man, the human soul and the soul's operations. Participating in playing a game is, according to Johan Huizinga's quoted passage: "free activity standing quite consciously outside 'ordinary' life," besides providing entertainment, it may well serve didactic purposes and teach the player useful skills and socially appropriate behaviour." A game as an organized social activity governed by strictly defined rules regulates the setting in which it is played, in a way it creates a conventional microcosm of its own. A sensible player participating in a game understands the rules and regulations governing its setting and process and can conclude from this knowledge to principles regulating the functioning of the human milieu in general. This means that participation in playing a game may help to acquire and develop "very useful knowledge of oneself".

The Cardinal and his interlocutor agree to examine the analogy obtaining between the ball used in the game and its movement toward the goal, that is toward the center of the playing ground and a human being and his/her progress toward the ultimate goal of all human beings. What features of shape, weight and texture must a ball have in order to smoothly move toward its goal? What intellectual and moral qualities must a human being possess in order to accomplish successfully his/her life's work and achieve the ultimate fulfillment of all his/her longing and desires? An attempt to find answer to these questions will be a good opportunity to explore the problems of anthropology and to expound Cusanus's conception of man. In fulfilling this task, the Cardinal in the dialogue *The Bowling-Game* will refer to some elements of the game of bowls as symbols of important anthropological notions.

It is man who manufactures balls for games; it is also a man, a player taking part in a game, who throws the ball and sets it in motion, which continues for a certain time under the influence of the impetus passed to it in the act of throwing. Impetus is a force which is invisible, yet wholly real, as can be inferred from its real and observable effect: the motion of

DOI: 10.4324/9781003310693-9

the ball. In this respect, impetus is very much like the human soul, which is also invisible in itself, but whose presence is noticeable by its effects, especially by the motion it imparts to its body, for the soul, being a substance capable of generating movement all by itself and of moving itself, and it is the unique source of the spontaneous movements of its body.[1] The ball with which a game of bowls is played is moved in different ways; in fact, its every movement is different from the others. A movement of the ball is the result of the force applied to it and the texture of the ground upon which it is rolling. The resultant effect of these two more or less accidentally combined forces is fairly unpredictable, and this introduces an element of unpredictability into the game and creates the risk for the players of failing to achieve the prescribed goal and thus losing the game. However, the Cardinal confidently assumes, if the ball used in the game of bowls was a perfect sphere, and the ground it is rolled upon ideally flat, its movement would never stop. A human being, by contrast, receives no impetus from outside; he/she has instead the source of the spontaneous motion within himself/herself; he/she moves owing to the soul, which is a principle dwelling in man and a force capable of moving itself. Cusanus's conception of the soul as self-motion is obviously a reminiscence of Plato's definition of the soul in *Phaedrus* (246a), where the soul's essence as self-movement is taken as the basis for postulating its immortality.

In a like way, Cusanus affirms movement to be an essential and not accidental property of the soul, and more precisely of the soul's most perfect part: the intellect. Being a Christian thinker, however, does not forget to add that the creator of the soul and thus the ultimate source of movement is God:

> However, God is the Creator of the substance. Many things partake of motion, so that they are moved because of a partaking of motion. Therefore, we arrive at one thing that is moved per se; and in order for it to be moved, motion does not come to it as an accident, and because of participation, but comes to it, rather, because of [that thing's] own essence. And [that thing] is the intellective soul, for the intellect moves itself.[2]

The human soul is present in the whole human body, and its power extends to every part of it; therefore, it is able to impart life, ability to feel and movement to the body as a whole and to its particular organs. The soul dwells in the body in a spiritual way: coextensive with the body, the soul is not divided in parts; it is one and whole in every part of it (just as God is whole and undivided in every point of space). The soul extends to the whole body its vital attention; therefore, it notices every change that takes place within it and accompanies these changes with a feeling of pain or joy; in this way, the soul participates in the affections and sufferings of its body, without being directly affected itself. Nicholas views the relationship obtaining between soul and body as a parallel-ism of a sort, with the soul, however, being the metaphysically superior element: in a true neoplatonic spirit, Cusanus affirms that the soul is in a sense the cause of its body, for it imposes the form of human body on the corporeal elements and maintains the harmonious and balanced relationship between them. Yet, for all the attention it lavishes on its body, the soul is better off on its own, freed from the encumbrance of its relation to the body. In particular, the soul better performs its cognitive functions when unaccompanied by the body, even if it is true that the bodily senses are the source of human knowledge of the material world:

> And so, the soul, as best it can, withdraws itself from the body in order better to think, to consider, and to determine. For the soul de-sires to be completely at liberty, in order to work freely. But this free power, which we call the rational soul, is stronger in proportion to its being free from bodily restrictions. Therefore, the soul is not more alive in the body than apart from it. Nor is it dissolved along with the dissolution of the body's harmony, or temperament, since it does not depend on the body's temperament, as does health. On the contrary, [the body's] temperament depends on the soul: if the soul does not exist, then neither does the temperament.[3]

So, the human soul is not confined in its cognitive activities to the sphere of the corporeal, nor does it totally depend on the collaboration with the senses: some of its cognitive powers, namely senses and imagina-tion, perform their functions in collaboration with bodily organs, while the higher faculties – reason and intelligence – are entirely independent of the body. All these faculties of the soul are different between themselves, yet all are grounded in one substance of the soul; the lower faculties exist as enfolded in the highest faculty, that is in the intellect/intelligence. This is a particular case illustrating the general law which governs the meta-physics of Nicholas's Universe: the lower and derivative is contained as enfolded in the higher and original reality:

> Likewise, too, the vegetative, perceptual, and imaginative powers that constitute the trigon that is called the brute animal's soul are of a more imperfect nature than they are in man, where, together with the very noble and very perfect intellectual power, they constitute the tetragon that is called man's soul. For lower things are present in higher things in accordance with the nature of the higher.[4]

The soul is by nature a reality that moves itself; it is self-motion; Cusanus finds evidence for this in the way of functioning of the higher faculties of the soul. The activity of reason can be represented as movement consisting of six subordinated motions: "it discriminates, abstracts, divides, and compounds" and makes rational inferences and reasons.[5] The functions of an intellective soul are three in number: thinking, consideration and determination. These three functions comprise the overall motion of the soul, which is circular, and reflexive, turning back upon itself and returning to its own starting point: thinking generates consideration, and thinking and consideration together lead to determination, which produces definition, an apt matter for a new process of thinking. All these stages comprise one dynamic movement which maintains itself in progressive motion. When trying to find the correct determination of what the soul is, that is the definition of the soul, a human being is engaged in thinking and considering:

> And when I inquire about the determination of the soul, as to what the soul is, then don't I also think about and consider? And I find that in this [mental activity] the soul moves itself with a circular movement, because that movement is turned back on itself. For when I think about thinking, [this] movement is circular and self-moving. And, hence, movement-of-soul, which is life, is perpetual, because it is a circular movement that is turned back on itself.[6]

These analyses clearly belong to the tradition started by Augustine's *Si fallor, sum* and continued by Eriugena's *intelligo me esse*.[7] The soul directly apprehends its own existence and its own essence: it knows itself, with the certainty of immediate evidence, to be indestructible substance of spiritual nature; it knows with perfect clarity its acts of cognition and willing and its own states. Because of the reflexive nature of the soul's knowledge, always accompanied by self-knowledge, Cusanus described the cognitive movement of the soul as circular. The three operations of the intellective soul (thinking, consideration and determination), different between themselves and yet inseparable from and necessarily presupposing one another, form together an image of the Divine Trinity impressed in the soul. The triune spiritual entity, the soul, in its unity and the triplicity of its intellective functions is the image of the triune God, and its mode of duration is the image of the divine mode: while God exists eternally, eternity being the mode of duration free from any kind of temporal succession, the soul exists perpetually or is perpetual, that is it endures forever, but is subject to some kind of temporal succession.[8] However, the Cardinal's partner in the dialogue, Prince John, raises a doubt concerning the unique and elevated status of man among the living creatures in nature: after all, animals, too, seem to "think-about, consider, and determine," so is man really so much different from them? The Cardinal's answer is very significant and points to a new aspect of human intellectual life, which consists in freedom:

> [The reason that animals are not rational is] that they lack free power, which is present in us. For example, when I wished to invent this game, I thought about, considered, and determined things which someone else did not think about or consider or determine. For each man is free to think about whatever he wishes to—and is free, like-wise, to consider and determine whatever he wishes to. Therefore, not all men think about the same thing, since each man has his own free spirit. But beasts are not like that. And so, they are impelled by nature toward the things that they do; and beasts of the same species engage in similar methods of hunting and build similar nests.[9]

As Jasper Hopkins observed in his commentary, Cusanus frequently mentions the freedom of choice and free will in his works, especially in his sermons, yet, as a rule, he does not subject these notions to care-ful scrutiny,[10] as he focuses on a description of the structure of human spiritual nature with particular attention being paid to human cogni-tive faculties. Nevertheless, in his account of the functioning of reason, and intellect, he presupposes certain freedom in human beings and, in particular, ability freely to choose among different possibilities, as be-comes evident in his attribution to reason and intellect of creativity and inventiveness. By contrast, the activity of animals, however spontane-ous it might appear, takes place within the rigid framework of necessity determined by their nature. This necessity is the work of and imposed by the Intelligence, which establishes the laws of nature, and it lies clearly beyond the cognitive grasp of animals themselves, although it can be understood by human beings, who are able to read in the book of nature, discover its laws and adjust their conduct to them. Nicholas draws a comparison, which may have been inspired by considerations of Thomas Aquinas[11]:

> Their nature (i.e. the nature of animals-AK) is moved by an intel-ligence. But [consider an analogy. Suppose that a monarchal] law-maker, moved by reason, has ordained the law (which moves his subjects) to be such as it is. [The subjects are moved] not [by] the rationale of the law, a rationale which is unknown to them, but [by] the imperial decree of their superior—an imperial decree that is bind-ing. In a similar way, a brute animal rather than being moved by the guidance-of-reason, of which the animal is ignorant, is moved by an

[intelligent] decree-of-nature that constrains it. And so, we see that all things of the same species are compelled and moved by a single specific motion as by an innate law of nature. [But] our spirit, which is regal and imperial, is not constrained by this force; otherwise, our spirit would not invent anything but would only comply with the impulse of its nature.[12]

The freedom of human spirit appears, among other things, in its exemption from the necessity imposed by nature and its ability to comprehend natural laws and to use them for its own freely chosen ends. This freedom becomes evident in those human actions and attitudes which either exceed the usual course and purposes of nature in the name of higher good, as abstinence and chastity, or clearly go against nature and constitute, in Nicholas's formulation, "sin against our nature," such as suicide.[13]

In order to properly use the potential of a human person, one ought to exercise one's faculty of free choice (*liberum arbitrium*), that is the ability to choose among diverse options in a given situation according to the judgment of right reason rather than in fulfilment of one's irrational desire. Freedom of choice is a priceless endowment of human nature that can ensure "the kingdom of man" freedom and autonomy, but only on the condition that man correctly recognizes the goal and the end of his/ her life and makes his/her decisions in the light of this recognition:

> For each man has free choice, i.e., the power to will and not to will; he knows [the difference between] virtue and vice, [between] what is honorable and what is dishonorable, what is just and what is unjust, what is laudable and what is reprehensible, what is glorious and what is shameful. And he knows that good is to be chosen, whereas evil is to be shunned; for he has within himself a king and a judge over those things which, since brute-animals are ignorant of them, belong to man qua man. And in regard to those things his noble kingdom is not at all subjected to the universe or to another creature—[something] not [true] in regard to those extrinsic goods which are called fortuitous, of which a man cannot have as many as he wishes to, because they are not subject to his free will, unlike the aforementioned immortal goods, which are subject to the will. For if his immortal soul wills to, it finds and freely chooses the immortal virtues as immortal nourishment for the soul's own life, even as the body's vegetative soul [seeks and finds] bodily food suitable for itself.[14]

The game of bowls comes in again as an apt image and symbol of the spiritual reality of forming one's ability to judge and choose correctly.

Let us take the motion of the ball thrown by a player toward the center of the playground as a symbol of the movement of our souls striving to reach the ultimate destiny of our lives, where we hope that "we may happily obtain rest in the Kingdom of Life together with Christ our King."[15]

A committed player ought to exercise his/her skills in setting the ball in motion so that it should reach the intended goal surely and quickly; a good player will also sharpen his/her ability to foresee possible impediments to the motion of the ball and take steps to avoid them or clear them out of the way; he/she will use all the means in his/her power to reduce the element of chance and maximize his/her own influence on the development of the game. He/she will be keenly aware of the risks involved in playing the game and in particular of the fact that once the ball is set in motion, its course cannot be changed, just as actions once performed and deed once committed in life cannot be annulled or undone.

The chief obstacles to successfully playing at the game, just as to successfully achieving the final goal in life, are bad inclinations of the human soul, natural or acquired, which should be straightened by exercise in practicing virtues.[16] Bad inclinations, if not overcome, generate bad habits, which are essential impediment in good conduct. Natural bad inclinations are the result of original sin, which deprived man of original justice and subjected his rational nature to the pernicious influence of irrational bodily desires.[17] Given the noxious presence of the legacy of original sin in the human constitution and in human life, a man, who is set upon successfully reaching the final goal of human life, should undertake the effort of forming his/her character by eliminating bad habits and replacing them with good ones, that is with virtues.

In this work upon the correction of our character, we ought constantly to bear in mind that it is the "inception of the motion" that lies within our power and not the motion' end. This desirable inception is the proper, that is virtuous, disposition to action.

> Therefore, it is necessary to pay attention to the inception of the motion. Consequently, a bad habit, which is a [kind of] movement, does not allow anyone to do well, unless, after it has been set aside, he causes a movement of virtue to result in a good habit. Therefore, if those who are running flaggingly finish the race poorly, then even if they regret it en route, they have to impute this result not to a disposition that is usually called fate or bad luck but to themselves, because, foolishly, they started off too fast.[18]

The prudent player will employ all the means in his/her power to ensure the success: he/she will assiduously perfect the skills and he/she will in advance plan the tactics in playing the game; yet he/she will never forget that the final result does not wholly depend on his/her efforts and that his/her own projects and actions, however shrewd and skillful, are not sufficient to decide the outcome of the game. Therefore, the prudent participant in that supreme game, which is no other than our life, will place his/her trust in the help from above. And he/she may well rest assured that the sincere and whole-hearted efforts in rectifying his/her natural inclinations and acquiring virtues will be assisted by God Himself:

> And God, who is being sought by means of man's movement, assists a good and persevering intention and perfects a good will. For God is the one who guides the believer and brings him to perfection and who by His omnipotent mercy repairs the weakened condition of the one who hopes in Him. Therefore, although a Christian who does his best is aware that his own bowling-ball is proceeding inconstantly, he is not confounded, because he trusts in God, who does not forsake those who hope in Him.[19]

The Cardinal in the dialogue, evidently an experienced master-teacher of wisdom and virtue), leads the way throughout the whole discussion of the game of bowls and its symbolism as a preparation for an exhortation addressed to his young interlocutor to undertake a serious effort of work on the formation of his character and habits, which is a necessary condition for an achievement of the most desirable end in life: the everlasting award for a successfully completed game of life. The Cardinal conducts his young friend along the path of spiritual exercise, which elevates a devoted human being to a point which opens a perspective upon the whole Universe and makes him aware of his own place within it with its possibilities, duties and dangers, and of his own vocation in the world, with its tasks, hopes and promises. This awareness of one's position within the universality of things carries with itself a challenge to undertake every effort necessary to fulfil one's calling and to make the hopes and promises involved therein come true. Yet in order to accomplish this, one has to subordinate one's whole life to that purpose, and one has to adopt a proper attitude to life and the important matters thereof. In this way, spiritual exercise involves a profound transformation of human life, changing one's habits and adopting a new attitude to life and its essential matters; in other words, it involves learning anew how to live.[20]

The consideration of the symbolism of the bowling game and the invitation to embark upon a life of spiritual exercise extended by the Cardinal to Prince John was not lost on the latter's cousin, Prince Albert, who, having acquainted himself with Book One of the dialogue, joined the Cardinal for a continuation of the exploration of the meaning of the game of bowls:

> Afterwards, admiring both the game and the book, I endeavored to understand something [of them] in accordance with my adolescent capability. But it seemed to me that you had not explained the symbolic meaning of the [ten] circles of the Region-of-Life. Therefore, I ask that Your Grace not despise in me this incapacity to understand so deep a symbolism. It will be the case that when I am more learned, I will remember what I have heard and, by the gift of God, will further learn.[21]

The life of philosophical spiritual exercises, to which the Cardinal introduces his pupils, involves the elements of both contemplation and action. The necessary foundation for the whole philosophical transformation of human life is theoretical contemplation of the structure of the whole Universe; in the dialogue, we are introduced into it by the consideration of the principles of the game. The insight into the foundation of the world not only brings satisfaction to the natural human desire to know but also ennobles man by elevating him/her above the current interests and his/her particular, aspectual point of view, and in this way, it opens the domain of higher values to human beings. Philosophical contemplation of the Universe opens the way for philosophical conversion, which leads to the awakening in human beings of spiritual intelligence,[22] which, in turn, is responsible for a complete reorientation of human lives:

> It is a concrete attitude and determinate lifestyle, which engages the whole of existence. The philosophical act is not situated merely on the cognitive level, but on that of the self and of being. It is a progress which causes us to be more fully, and makes us better. It is a conversion which turns our entire life upside down, changing the life of the person who goes through it. It raises the individual from an inauthentic condition of life, darkened by unconsciousness and harassed by worry, to an authentic state of life, in which he attains self-consciousness, an exact vision of the world, inner peace, and freedom.[23]

To this fundamentally correct description of the philosophical conversion, Cusanus would add an essentially Christian element: it is God through His intervention that brings to completion the process of human growth toward perfection and with His grace comes to the aid of those who put their trust and hope in Him. Since original sin continues to exert its devastating influence on all human beings, impairing the nature and proper functioning of their faculties, no human being, left to their own devices, is able to achieve the ultimate goal of human life.

Therefore, the path to a full realization of humanity's potential leads not only through the development and integration of human cognitive and volitional powers under the direction of reason but also through the growth of the three theological virtues of faith, hope and charity:

> Therefore, if the "bowling-ball" of your person is impelled by the spirit of faith, then (1) it is guided by steadfast hope and (2) by love it is bound to Christ, who will lead you with Him unto Life. But such is impossible for an unbeliever. *John*: I see the following to be altogether certain: He who does not believe in Christ as the Son of God clings to the world and does not look forward to a better life. By contrast, a believer rejoices in adversity, because he knows that a glorious death will lead to immortal life.[24]

The person of Jesus Christ stands in the center of the game of our lives as the goal and fulfilment, but it is also the way that leads to that center, both through favorable circumstances and, importantly, through adversities. The game of bowls receives an interpretation as an image of a liturgical mystery in which the principal actors are Christ and His Church. As was already observed above, liturgical performance is said not only to represent the sacred mysteries but also to make them present and operative *hic et nunc* by representing them. During a liturgical ceremony, Jesus Christ is said to be present and exert His salvific and integrating power through sacramental signs[25] in order to transform the selves of the faithful in the image of His Own Self. A mature participant of the game of life will know that the only right option for him/her is to surrender to that transforming Influence and let himself/herself be formed in the image and likeness of that Divine Player, rather than follow the promptings of the ephemeral human ego.[26]

This inner transformation of a human ego is accomplished above all by virtue of the theological virtue of faith, whose work within a human being is to renew the divine image impressed in man in the very act of creation, and the effect of this renovation is to purify human intellect and enable it to experience the vision of God. In his sermon CCLXXI composed in 1457 and delivered in Brixen, Cusanus mentioned that ability of human intellect to experience the vision of God:

> But an intellect that does not know itself is without intellectual life, for an intellect's understanding is its living. Hence, if the intellect is to attain to life in order, indeed, to understand itself and to be alive with an intellectual life, then it is necessary that its origin be revealed to it. But who can reveal its origin to it except Him who (1) knows the Father and (2) knows the Intellect which is Creator and (3) is the Exemplar

of the Father's creating—namely, the Son and Word of the Father? For no one knows the Father qua Father-who-is Fatherhood except the Son qua Son-who-is-Sonship. Therefore, it is evident that there can be made no revelation of the truth to the [human] intellect qua image of God except by the Exemplar—i.e., by the Word *Haec Omnia Dabo Tibi* through which the intellect was created. But if a revelation is to be made to the created intellect, it is necessary that the [created] intellect be capable of faith; i.e., [it is necessary] that it be able to believe. For unless it could believe the one who reveals, how could there be revelation to it? Hence, the power of believing is present in the intellect. Through this free power [the intellect both] can believe the one who reveals and can learn. And if the one who reveals at that time is the Word of God and if [the intellect] believes Him: then, without doubt, [the intellect] can by faith attain life, namely, the vision of the Father—[a vision] that brings happiness, as stated previously.[27]

The game of human life, like the bowling game, has a set goal, which all the players try to achieve. Unlike the latter game, however, the participation in the game of life is not an object of voluntary choice: we find out that we are already taking part in it when we start thinking about it, and we cannot refuse further participation, although we can refuse acceptance of certain conditions imposed by the game. Nevertheless, like the players in bowling, we all strive to achieve some objectives and we all have an idea, albeit hazy and unclear, of a final goal, which, once achieved, will satisfy all our desires and fulfil all our needs. Traditionally, this ultimate end of all human endeavors has been called happiness, so we might say that we take happiness to be the final goal of the game of our lives. But the Cardinal in the dialogue, enlightened by the wisdom emanating from Christian faith, knows that ultimate and perfect happiness can only be had in seeing God, so he affirms that the ultimate purpose of that all-encompassing game which is our life is seeing God and by that vision being assimilated to Him. The motion toward this goal starts when human intellect, in which all other human faculties are enfolded, looks into its own depths and impressed discovers there the "concept of concepts," the innate, unclear and indistinct notion of God. As already observed above, this "first thing known" is the first and necessary foundation for all human thinking and knowing; it is presupposed and operative in all human mental functions, even if human beings, as is most often the case, remain unaware of its presence and function. However, once we sincerely and wholeheartedly enter into the spirit of our life's game, we are taken on a journey of discoveries, which progressively reveals to us the hidden foundation of our being, knowing and happiness, and thus, we will become aware of this primary notion of God present and working in us. It is precisely this notion that gives us the foretaste of God, an experience that inspires us to seek ever more of God, His greatness, goodness and beauty, and in this way sends us on a journey toward the fullness of happiness. Yet, as already noted above, although we all must somehow take part in the game of our lives, we may refuse to engage the full potential of our minds and hearts in it; in particular, we may fail to embrace whole-heartedly and single-mindedly God as the single absolute goal of our life game. The Cardinal distinguishes three kinds of participants in the life game, depending on how much they engage in the play and the nature of their engagement:

> Therefore, each Christian must contemplate how it is that (1) some men have no hope of another life; and they move their bowling-ball [only] here on earth. (2) Other men have the hope of happiness, but they struggle to arrive at that [eternal] life by means of their own powers and laws, apart from Christ; and by following the powers of their mind and by keeping the commandments of their prophets and teachers, they cause their own ball to run toward high matters; yet, their bowling-balls do not reach the Kingdom of Life. (3) There is a third group of men, who embrace the Way which Christ, the only-begotten Son of God, preached and walked; they direct themselves toward the Center, where there is the throne of the King-of-Powers and of the Mediator between God and men. And by following in the footsteps of Christ, they impel their bowling-ball by means of a central pathway; [and] they alone obtain a mansion in the Kingdom of Life.[28]

Only the last named category of players, the Christians, will reach the ultimate goal of the play, for only true Christians follow in the footsteps of Him, who is both the Way and the very Goal of the game of life. The person of Jesus Christ is the paradigmatic Coin, whose likeness is impressed on every single coin put in circulation by God-the Supreme Minter, but being one with His Father, Jesus Christ is the Supreme Minter himself. Every participant in the game of life is one of the many coins forged by the Divine Minter, but he/she is also a banker, who evaluates, uses and circulates other coins, manages financial resources and by careful investment should increase the value of the fund of created goods left at his/her disposal, that is to enlarge the dominion of the Kingdom of God on earth. According to Devin Singh,

> The language of money, currency, and coinage is employed in patristic thought both to depict human nature and salvation and to describe Christ and his work. Humans are portrayed as coins, impressed with the image of their creator. This image has been

eroded by sin but is renewed by a fresh stamping or reminting by the savior. Christ is the paradigmatic image, the stamp used to make impressions of the *imago Dei* on humanity. He is thus incarnated as the chief coin, as the governing materialization of this ideal monetary image. Soteriological language of reminting and reissuing coins coincides with the widespread ancient practice of monarchs declaring their reign through new coin types. The fresh reminting of humanity thus proclaims the inbreaking kingdom of God. To be reminted and restamped in the divine image is as much a divine assertion of sovereignty as it is an act of redemption for lost humanity. The submerged idea of Christ as the currency of God, manifesting the redemptive economy of the Father, provides a structuring principle for explanations of Christ's work and the values of God's kingdom.[29]

Every human being is part of that divinely instituted "monetary system" and yet called upon to participate in the management of it, for it is only as an active collaborator in the work of maintaining and enlarging the divine order of creation that he can achieve satisfaction of his yearnings and fulfilment. One can say that the vocation of a human being is to multiply the value of the "human capital" established by God, by means of increasing the value of the coin that is himself, in making it a true image of God and the God-created Universe, and in this way contributing to the work of Redemption.[30] In the work *On Surmises*, Cusanus observes:

> Since [man] surmises that all things are attained by the senses or by reason or by intellect, and since he sees that these powers of his are enfolded within his oneness, he supposes that he can proceed unto all things in a human way. For man is god, but not unqualifiedly, since he is man; therefore, he is a human god.[31]

In this way, a whole-hearted acceptance of one's part in the divinely instituted game of life and a conscientious performance of one's duties as a divinely appointed manager of created valuable resources, by increasing the value of the fund of goods left in the hands of human managers-bankers, result in magnifying God's glory, for God's glory is best proclaimed by the true happiness and perfect condition of His creatures.

There is, however, one aspect of spiritual exercises to which philosophy invites, which may seem forbidding, namely learning to die. Since its birth in antiquity, philosophy has promised to teach human beings how to preserve peace of mind, impassible attitude and even cheerful disposition in the face of the great evils of life, such as pain, illness, hostility of others, loss of dear ones, loss of material goods and, finally, death. Rather than shunning the adversities and calamities inseparable from human existence, it invited the philosophically minded to confront and bear them courageously. The instruction given by the Cardinal in the dialogue to his young friends does not pass over the dark sides of life in silence but sets them in the perspective of the salvation promised by religion and the limited and only relative value of material goods. A committed player participating in the game of life, conscious of the surpassing value of the final reward he expects, not only bears with equanimity but even "rejoices in adversity." The lesson he has to receive in the art of dying is the lesson of dying to his irrational bodily desires and egoistic attitudes.

> If, then, the soul is [created] by God in order to attain a vision of the glory of His majesty, then the soul has a body only in order to apprehend God's visible works, to the end [of obtaining a vision] of God's glory. And so, [the soul] ought not to be attached to the flesh or to visible things and ought not to give itself over to corruptible desires but ought in all respects to turn to magnifying the glory of the Great God. And thereby [it ought] to transfer itself by means of visible things unto the Invisible God, in order that God may be the intended End. God is Goodness itself, which is desired by all.[32]

Thus, the philosophical spiritual exercise, into which the Cardinal invites his young pupils in *The Bowling Game* with the aid of the consideration of the symbolism implicit in the game, turns out to be an exercise in passing from the perception of concrete, visible reality of the human experience to contemplation of "invisible qualities" of God (cf. Rom 1:20) and a consideration of His glory.

Notes

1 Cf. LG I, 25, p. 1193. Impetus' theory was formulated in the 14th century by John Buridan. His disciple was Marsilius of Inghen (1340–1396), *magister* at the University of Heidelberg. Cf. JACK ZUPKO, JOHN Buridan (c.1300–after 1358), 1998, doi:10.4324/9780415249126-B022-1. Routledge Encyclopedia of Philosophy, Taylor and Francis, https://www.rep.routledge.com/articles/biographical/buridan-john-c-1300-after-1358/v-1.
2 LG I, 25, p. 1193.
3 LG I, 31, p. 1197.
4 LG I, 39, p. 1200.
5 Cf. LG I, 28, p. 1195.
6 LG I, 32, p. 1197.
7 Cf. AGNIESZKA KIJEWSKA. "Human Mind as Manifestation of God's Mind in Eriugena's Philosophy." *Anuario Filosófico*, 49, n. 2, 2016, pp. 361–384.
8 Cf. LG I, 37, p. 1200; I, 33, p. 1197.

9 LG I, 34, p. 1198.
10 LG, p. 1258, footnote 84.
11 Cf. GIORGIO AGAMBEN. *The Kingdom and the Glory*, trans. by L. Chiesa, M. Mandarni, Stanford University Press, Stanford, CA, 2011, pp. 84–97.
12 LG I, 35, pp. 1198–1199.
13 LG I, 36, p. 1199.
14 LG I, 58, p. 1211.
15 LG I, 60, p. 1212.
16 LG I, 54, p. 1209.
17 Cusanus very rarely touches on the topic of original sin. Cf. S-1 VI, 1, 5, p. 109.
18 LG I, 56, p. 1210.
19 LG I, 59, p. 1212.
20 Cf. PIERRE HADOT. *Philosophy as a Way of Life : Spiritual Exercises* from Socrates to Foucault, ed. by A. Davidson, trans. by M. Chase, Blackwell, Malden, MA 1995, pp. 82–89.
21 LG II, 61, p. 1213.
22 This is also an important issue in contemporary psychology. Cf. DANAH ZOHAR, IAN MARSHALL. *Spiritual Intelligence. The Ultimate Intelligence*, Bloomsbury, London-New York-Berlin-Sydney, 2012 (e-book), lok. 57: "By SQ [spiritual quantum – A.K.] I mean the intelligence with which we can place our actions and our lives in a wider, richer, meaning-giving context, the intelligence with which we can assess that one course of action or one life-path is more meaningful than another. SQ is the necessary foundation for the effective functioning of both IQ and EQ. It is our ultimate intelligence."
23 HADOT. *Spiritual Exercises,* p. 83.
24 LG I, 53, p. 1208.
25 Cf. PETER J. CASARELLA. "Sacraments," in: *Introducing Nicholas of Cusa. A Guide to a Renaissance Man,* ed. Ch. M. Bellito, Th. M. Izbicki, G. Christianson, Paulist Press, New York-Mahwah, NJ, 2004, pp. 347–372.
26 Cf. JOHANNES HOFF, *The Analogical Turn*, p. 22: "However, in Cusa's view the liturgical practice of praise was more than a gesture of grateful submission to the greater glory of God. It had a constitutive, gnoseological function: only the praise of God can preserve our truth-seeking mind from the analytic pretensions of a disoriented rationality for its own sake."
27 S-3 *All These Things I Will Give You*, 5, pp. 128–129.
28 LG I, 51, pp. 1207–1208.
29 DEVIN SINGH. *Divine Currency*. The Theological Power of Money in the West, Stanford University Press, Stanford, CA, 2018, p. 105.
30 Cf. E. ELEONORE STUMP. *Atonement*, Oxford University Press, Oxford, 2018, p. 23.
31 DC, II, 14, 143, p. 236.
32 S-2 CCII: *Spiritu Ambulate* 5, p. 401.

10 Concluding remarks

Nicholas of Cusa's remarkable work, *The Bowling-Game*, represents to the reader a picture of life devoted to spiritual exercise under the direction of philosophical wisdom; in its essence, this work is an invitation extended to the reader to embark upon the life of conscious spiritual effort, a philosophical game, which makes a human being an active participant in the divine *oikonomia*. The divine economy, in turn, is the realization of God's plan for the fallen humanity to reunite it again with Himself; it is, as St. Paul says, the implementation of "the mystery of His will, according to His kind intention," "with a view to an economy of the fullness" (Ef 1:9–10). At the end of the way of life devoted to spiritual exercise is found the perfect fulfilment of the human capacity for happiness, the perfect flourishing of human nature, which can be also described as atonement. Eleonore Stump explains the meaning of the word as used in this context:

> 'Atonement' is a word that was devised to express the idea that the *at onement* is a making one of things that were previously not at one, namely, God and human beings. So if the *at onement* is the solution to a problem, then, it seems, the problem should be thought as the absence of unity or oneness between God and human beings.[1]

So, the central problem of man can be defined in terms of lost unity, unity with himself/herself, with other human beings, and with God. But how can man regain that lost inner unity (*onement*) and the unity with the world and God? What caused the break between man and God, the split within man himself and the alienation of man from the surrounding world, the feeling of having been thrown into an unfriendly and incomprehensible world? Let us follow Stump's explanation:

> The post-Fall human condition is therefore a serious obstacle to flourishing, in one's own life and in one's relations to other persons. And' of course, for all these same reasons, the human proneness to

DOI: 10.4324/9781003310693-10

moral wrongdoing is also a major source of distance from God. The post-Fall human condition that wards off closeness between human persons will ward off closeness between human person and God, too. I do not mean that a perfectly good God turns his back on human beings in consequence of their sinfulness. (...) part of what it is for God to be perfectly good is for God always to desire union with human beings. But union is reciprocal, and it requires mutual closeness.[2]

If having lost union with God is man's central problem, his/her overriding concern should be to regain that lost unity. Scholastic theology in the Middle Ages proposed various theories of the Fall and the Salvation effected by Jesus Christ and the way it opened for the reunion of human beings with their Maker. Stump distinguishes two main types of theories of the return of man to union with God; she calls these types Anselmian and Thomistic respectively. The Anselmian doctrine lays the stress upon God's justice and interprets original sin as an offence of God, which calls for atonement. Yet man on his/her own is unable to offer adequate satisfaction for this offence.

Interpretation of the doctrine of the *at onement* of the Anselmian kind consequently tend to emphasize the passion and death of Christ as paying the penalty for human beings, or serving to repay the moral debt for human beings, or constituting a penance for human sin (...). On interpretations of this kind, God is not only perfectly just but also infinitely merciful; and so he brings it about that he himself endures the human penalty, or pays the human debt in full, or makes the requisite penance, by assuming human nature as the incarnate Christ and in that nature enduring the penalty or paying the debt or providing the penance which would otherwise have had to be imposed on or exacted from human beings.[3]

On this interpretation, Christ is the coin with which the debt contracted by man to God-the Father is paid. By putting this coin, bearing the impressed likeness of God Himself, in circulation, God extends His dominion and redeems man from the slavery of sin. However, man remains free to accept or refuse this coin or else to "bury it in the ground."

The other group of doctrines of redemption, that of the Thomist stamp, emphasizes human inclination to evil and frailty of human will as the causes of original sin. The salvific work of Christ entails above all reinforcing the insufficient strength of man, as Stump relates:

On Aquina's view, without violating human free will, God's operative grace produces in a human person a will for a will that wills the good; and God's cooperative grace works with that partially healed human will to increase in it the strength for willing the good. For Aquina's, Christ's passion and death produced many good effects for human being. But the main one is that of providing the grace that heals the defect in human will through the process of justification and sanctification. By his passion and death, Christ provided this healing grace to human beings who are united to him in faith and love.[4]

I believe, the Thomist conception of *at onement* is particularly close to the ideas of Nicholas of Cusa, who thought that a Christian participant in the game of life (the third category of players) should combine his personal efforts in straightening his/her natural inclinations with reliance on God's aid as obtainable through practicing the theological virtues of faith, hope and charity, which alone can guide one along the way leading to the Kingdom of life. By exercising intellectual faculties through study and contemplation of the Universe, by cultivating moral virtues, and by strengthening the will with the help of divine grace, human being comes to resemble Christ and becomes a coin forged by God and put in circulation in the divine oikonomia.

These committed Christian participants in the game of life, who are ready to undertake every effort to make themselves and the world better and to include their personal strivings in the mysterious global work of the divine economy in the world, may build a human environment formed and permeated by values, which are both divinely inspired and authentically human, which may put both theological and economical thinking on new paths of development. In the words of Kathryn Tanner, these new impulses for theology and economics should be oriented to fundamental values:

> One common strategy for extending the economic relevance of Christianity beyond this history of rather limited direct comment and for enhancing Christianity's systematic economic import is to highlight fundamental Christian values. The focus becomes such Christian mainstays as love for neighbour, respect for the dignity of the human person, and repudiation of envy and greed in relations with others. Any one of those values might affect the whole of life, anchoring and centering it, and therefore help give a Christian economic perspective a systematic cast.[5]

For indeed, every human being faces the fundamental choice: he/she may either contribute to the growth of the "capital" of good in the world or become part of the forces of disintegration and destruction. There is really only one way leading to the Union: *at onement*.

St. Ignatius of Antioch in his *Letter to Magnesians* put it in clear and concise words:

> Seeing then that there is an end to all, that the choice is between two things, death and life, and that each is to go to his own place; for, just as there are two coinages, the one of God, the other of the world, and each has its own stamp impressed on it, so the unbelievers bear the stamp of this world, and the believers the stamp of God the Father in love through Jesus Christ, and unless we willingly choose to die through him in his passion, his life is not in us.[6]

Notes

1 ELEONORE STUMP. *Atonement*, Oxford University Press, Oxford, 2018, p. 15.
2 There, p. 17.
3 There p. 22.
4 There, p. 23.
5 KATHRYN TANNER. *Economy of Grace*, Fortress Press, Minneapolis, 2005, p. 3.
6 IGNATIOUS OF ANTIOCH. "Letter to the Magnesians," V, in: *Readings in World Christian History*, vol. 1: *Earliest Christianity to 1453*, eds. John W. Coakley, A. Sterk, Orbis Books, Maryknoll, New York, 2004, p. 13.

Bibliography

Primary sources

ALAIN, DE LILLE. *Règles de théologie*, ed. F. Hudry, Les Editions du Cerf, Paris, 1995.

ANSELM of CANTERUBRY. *Proslogion*, trans. by J. Hopkins and H. Richardson, in: *Complete Philosophical and Theological Treatises of Anselm of Canterbury*, The Arthur J. Banning Press, Minneapolis, 2000, pp. 88–112 (proslogion.pdf [jasper-hopkins.info]).

BOETHIUS. *Consolation of Philosophy*, trans. by Joel C. Relihan, Hackett Publishing Company, Indianapolis, Cambridge, 2001.

BOÉCE. *Institution Arithmétique*, ed. J.-Y. Gillaumin, Les Belles Lettres, Paris, 1995.

BOETHIUS. "How substances can be good in virtue of their existence without being absolute goods." in: *The Theological Tractates*, trans. by H. F. Stewart, E. K. Rand, Heinemann, London, Harvard University Press, Cambridge MA, 1968, pp. 38–51.

CALCIDIUS. *On Plato's "Timaeus."* trans. by J. Magee, Harvard University Press, Cambridge, MA, London, 2016.

IGNATIOUS OF ANTIOCH. "Letter to the Magnesians," V, in: *READINGS IN WORLD CHRISTIAN HISTORY*, vol. 1: *Earliest Christianity to 1453*, eds. John W. Coakley, A. Sterk, Orbis Books, Maryknoll, New York, 2004, pp. 12–14.

NICHOLAS OF CUSA. *A defence of Learned Ignorance*, in: *Nicholas of Cusa's Debate with John Wenck*, trans. by J. Hopkins, The Arthur J. Banning Press, Minneapolis, 1981, pp. 459–492 (Apologia12-2000.pdf [jasper-hopkins. info]).

———. *Compendium*, trans. by Jasper Hopkins, in: *Nicholas of Cusa on Wisdom and Knowledge*, The Arthur J. Banning Press, Minneapolis, 1996, pp. 1386–1419 (Compendium12-2000.pdf [jasper-hopkins.info]).

———. *Concerning the Loftiest Level of Contemplative Reflection*, trans. by J. Hopkins, in: *Nicholas of Cusa: Metaphysical Speculations*, The Arthur J. Banning Press, Minneapolis, 1998, pp. 1423–1442 (DeApice12-2000.pdf [jasper-hopkins.info]).

———. *Nicholas of Cusa's Didactic Sermons: A Selection*, The Arthur J. Bannings Press, Loveland, Colorado, 2008. FinalSelectSermons front matter.qxp (jasper-hopkins.info).

——. *Nicholas of Cusa's Early Sermons: 1430-1441*, trans. by J. Hopkins, The Arthur J. Banning Press, Loveland, Colorado, 2003 (CusaEarlySerintro.pdf [jasper-hopkins.info]).

——. *Nicholas of Cusa's Last Sermons (1457-1463)*, trans. by J. Hopkins, 2011 (Preface & Introduction [jasper-hopkins.info]).

——. *On Actualized-possibility*, trans. by J. Hopkins, University of Minnesota Press, Minneapolis, 1978.

——. *On being a Son of God*, in: *A Miscellany on Nicholas of Cusa*, trans. by J. Hopkins, The Arthur J. Banning Press, Minneapolis, 1994, pp. 341–369 (DeFiliatione12-2000.pdf [jasper-hopkins.info]).

——. *On [intellectual] eyeglasses*, trans. by J. Hopkins, in: *Nicholas of Cusa: Metaphysical Speculations*, The Arthur J. Banning Press, Minneapolis, 1998, pp. 792–838 (DeBeryllo12-2000.pdf [jasper-hopkins.info]).

——. *On Learned Ignorance*, trans. by J. Hopkins, 2nd ed., The Arthur J. Banning Press, Minneapolis, 1985 (DI-I-12-2000.pdf [jasper-hopkins.info]).

——. *On Non-other*, trans. by J. Hopkins, in: *Nicholas of Cusa on God as Not-other. A Translation and an Appraisal of De Li Non Aliud*, 3rd edition, The Arthur J. Banning Press, Minneapolis, 1987, pp. 1108–1178 (NA12-2000. pdf [jasper-hopkins.info]).

——. *On Peaceful Unity of Faith*, trans. by J. Hopkins, 2nd ed., The Arthur J. Banning Press, Minneapolis 1994, pp. 633–676 (DePace12-2000.pdf [jasper-hopkins.info]).

——. *On the Pursuit of Wisdom*, trans. by J. Hopkins, in: *Nicholas of Cusa: Metaphysical Speculations*, The Arthur J. Banning Press, Minneapolis, 1998, pp. 1278–1381 (VS12-2000.pdf [jasper-hopkins.info]).

——. *On Surmises*, in: *Nicholas of Cusa: Metaphysical Speculations: Volume Two*, ed. J. Hopkins, The Arthur J. Banning Press, Minneapolis, 2000, pp. 163–297 (DeConi12-2000 [jasper-hopkins.info]).

——. *The Bowling-Game*, trans. by J. Hopkins, in: *Nicholas of Cusa: Metaphysical Speculations: Volume Two*, The Arthur J. Banning Press, Minneapolis, 2000. p. 1182–1274 (DeLudo12-2000.pdf [jasper-hopkins.info]).

——. *The Catholic Concordance*, trans. by P. E. Sigmund, Cambridge University Press, Cambridge, 1991.

——. *The Layman on Mind*, trans. by J. Hopkins, in: *Nicholas of Cusa on Wisdom and Knowledge*, The Arthur J. Banning Press, Minneapolis, 1996, pp. 531–601 (DeMente12-2000.pdf [jasper-hopkins.info]).

——. *The Layman on Wisdom*, trans. by J. Hopkins, in: *Nicholas of Cusa on Wisdom and Knowledge*, The Arthur J. Banning Press, Minneapolis, 1996, pp. 497–526 (DeSap12-2000.pdf [jasper-hopkins.info]).

——. *The Vision of God*, trans. by J. Hopkins, in: *Nicholas of Cusa's Dialectical Mysticism*, 3rd ed., The Arthur J. Banning Press, Minneapolis, 1985, pp. 679–743 (dialectical mysticism q 12-2000.qxd [jasper-hopkins.info]).

PIUS II, *Pamiętniki*, ed. A. von Heck, trans. by J. Wojtkowski, Biblioteca Apostolica Vaticana, Marki, 2005.

Plato, *The Republic*, trans. by G. M. A. Grube, Hackett Publishing Company, Indianapolis, 1974.

THIERRY OF CHARTRES. *Commentaries on Boethius by Thierry of Chartres and His School*, ed. N. M. Häring, Pontifical Institute of Mediaeval Studies, Toronto, 1971.

Secondary sources

AERTSEN, IAN A. *Medieval Philosophy and the Transcendentals. The Case of Thomas Aquinas*, Brill, Leiden-New York-Köln, 1996.

AGAMBEN, GIORGIO. *Creation and Anarchy. The Work of Art and the Religion of Capitalism*, trans. by A. Kotsko, Stanford University Press, Stanford, CA, 2019.

————. *The Kingdom and the Glory*, trans. by L. Chiesa, M. Mandarni, Stanford University Press, Stanford, CA, 2011.

ALBERTINI, TAMARA. "Mathematics and Astronomy." in: *Introducing Nicholas of Cusa. A Guide to a Renaissance Man*, eds. Ch. M. Bellito, Th. M. Izbicki, G. Christianson, Paulist Press, New York-Mahwah, NJ, 2004, pp. 373–406.

ALBERTSON, DAVID. *Mathematical Theologies. Nicholas of Cusa and the Legacy of Thierry of Chartres*, Oxford University Press, Oxford, 2014.

ASPRAY, SILVIANNE. "Performative Finitude: Theological Language and the God-World Relationship in Nicholas of Cusa 'De Non Aliud'." *International Journal of Systematic Theology*, 24, n.2, 2022, pp. 173–190.

BIECHLER, JAMES E. "Interreligious Dialogue." in: *Introducing Nicholas of Cusa. A Guide to a Renaissance Man*, eds. Ch. M. Bellito, Th. M. Izbicki, G. Christianson, Paulist Press, New York-Mahwah, NJ, 2004, pp. 270–296.

BINMORE, KEN, *Game Theory. A Very Short Introduction*, Oxford University Press, Oxford, 2007.

BIRKENMAJER, ALEXANDER. *Le rôle joué par les médecins et les naturalistes dans la réception d'Aristote au XII et XIIIe siècle*, Imprimerie Współczesna, Varsovie, 1930.

BLUMENBERG, HANS. *The Legitimacy of the Modern Age (Studies in Contemporary German Social Thought)*, The MIT Press, Cambridge, MA, 1985.

BOND, HUGH LAWRENCE. "Mystical Theology." in: *Introducing Nicholas of Cusa. A Guide to a Renaissance Man*, eds. Ch. M. Bellito, Th. M. Izbicki, G. Christianson, Paulist Press, New York-Mahwah, NJ, 2004, pp. 205–231.

————. "Nicholas of Cusa from Constantinople to *Learned Ignorance*: The Historical Matrix for the formation of *De docta ignorantia*." in: *Reform, Representation*, eds. H. L. Bond, G. Christianson, Routledge, London, New York, 2011, pp. 195–225.

————. "The Journey of the Soul to God in Nicholas of Cusa's 'De ludo globi'." in: *Nicholas of Cusa. In Search of God and Wisdom*, eds. G. Christianson, Th. Izbicki, Brill, Leiden, 1991, pp. 71–86.

BUKAŁA, MARCIN. "Scholastic Concepts Concerning the Idea of Economic Value." in: *I Beni di questo mondo. Teorie etico-economiche nel laboratorio dell'Europa medieval*, ed. R. Lambertini, L. Sileo, Fédération Internationale des Instituts d'Etudes Médiévales, Porto, 2010, pp. 349–357.

CASARELLA, PETER J. "Nicholas of Cusa and the Power of the Possible." *American Catholic Philosophical Quarterly*, 64, n.1, 1990, pp. 7–34.

————. "Sacraments." in: *Introducing Nicholas of Cusa. A Guide to a Renaissance Man*, eds. Ch. M. Bellito, Th. M. Izbicki, G. Christianson, Paulist Press, New York-Mahwah, NJ, 2004, pp. 347–372.

CASSIRER, ERNST. *The Individual and the Cosmos in Renaissance Philosophy*, trans. by M. Domandi, Dover Publications, INC., Mineola, New York, 2000.

CERTEAU, MICHEL DE. "The Gaze. Nicholas of Cusa." trans. by C. Porter, *Diacritics*, 17, 1987, pp. 2–38.

COUNET, JEAN-MICHEL. "Introduction." in: Nicolas de Cues, *Les Conjectures*, Les Belles Lettres, Paris, 2011, pp. X–CLVII.

———. *Matématiques et dialectique chez Nicolas de Cues*, Librairie Vrin, Paris, 2000.

CRANZ, EDWARD F. "Development in Cusanus?" in: *Nicholas of Cusa and the Renaissance*, eds. Th. M. Izbicki, G. Christianson, Ashgate, Variorum, 2003, pp. 1–18.

———. "Reason and Beyond Reason." in: *Nicholas of Cusa and the Renaissance*, eds. Th. M. Izbicki, G. Christianson, Ashgate, Variorum, 2003, pp. 19–30.

CUOZZO, GIANLUCA. "Coincidence des opposes," in: *Encyclopédie des mystiques rhénans. D'Eckhart à Nicolas de Cues et leur réception*, ed. M.-A. Vannier, Cerf, Paris, 2011, pp. 253–257.

DAVIS, BRIAN, "Anselm and the ontological argument." in: *The Cambridge Companion to Anselm*, eds. B. Davies, B. Leftow, Cambridge University Press, Cambridge, 2004, pp. 157–178.

DEMPSEY, MICHAEL T. "Providence." in: *The Routledge Handbook of Economic Theology*, ed. S. Schwarzkopf, Routledge, London-New York, 2020, pp. 19–27.

DOMARADZKI, MIKOŁAJ. "The Beginnings of Greek Allegoresis." *The Classical World*, 110, n. 3, 2017, pp. 299–321.

DUCLOW, DONALD F. "Coinciding in the Margins: Cusanus glosses Eriugena." in: *Eriugena-Cusanus*, ed. A. Kijewska, R. Majeran, H. Schwaetzer, Wydawnictwo KUL, Lublin, 2011, pp. 83–103.

———. "Life and Works." in: *Introducing Nicholas of Cusa. A Guide to a Renaissance Man*, eds. Ch. M. Bellito, Th. M. Izbicki, G. Christianson, Paulist Press, New York-Mahwah, NJ, 2004, pp. 25–56.

DUPRÉ, WILHELM. "Docte ignorance (thème)," in: *Encyclopédie des mystiques rhénans. D'Eckhart à Nicolas de Cues et leur réception*, ed. M.-A. Vannier, Cerf, Paris, 2011, pp. 394–400.

ENCYCLOPEDIE DES MYSTIQUES RHENANS. D'Eckhart à Nicolas de Cues et leur réception, ed. M.-A. Vannier, Cerf, Paris, 2011.

EULER, WALTER A. "L'image de l'islam à la fin du Moyen Âge. La correspondance entre Jean de Ségovie et Nicolas de Cues." in: *Nicolas de Cues et l'islam*, ed. H. Pasqua, Peeters, Louvain-la-Neuve, Louvain-Paris, 2013, pp. 9–20.

FAUSTINO, MARTA, FERRARO, GIANFRANCO (eds.). *The Late Foucault. Ethical and Political Questions*, Bloomsbury Academic, London-New York-Oxford-New Delhi-Sydney, 2020.

FÜHRER, MARKUS. *Echoes of Aquinas in Cusanus's Vision of Man*, Lexington Books, Lanham-Boulder-New York-Toronto-Plymouth, 2014 (e-book).

GERSH, STEPHEN. "Omnipresence in Eriugena. Some Reflections on Augustino-Maximian Element in 'Periphyseon'." in: *Eriugena. Studien zu seinen Quellen, Vorträge des II. Internationalen Eriugena-Colloquiums*, ed. W. Beierwaltes, Carl Winter Universitätsverlag, Heidelberg, 1980, pp. 55–74.

GRONDKOWSKA, BARBARA. *Znaki i symbole. Filozofia w kazaniach Mikołaja z Kuzy [Signs and Symbols. Philosophy in Cusanus' Sermons]*, Towarzystwo Naukowe KUL Press, Lublin, 2018.

HADOT, PIERRE. *Philosophy as a Way of Life: Spiritual Exercises from Socrates to Foucault*, ed. A. Davidson, trans. by M. Chase, Blackwell, Malden, MA 1995.
———. *What is Ancient Philosophy?* trans. by M. Chase, The Belknap Press of Harvard University Press, Cambridge MA, London, 2004.
HENDRIX, SCOTT H. "Nicholas of Cusa's Ecclesiology Between Reform and Reformation." in: *Nicholas of Cusa on Christ and the Church*, eds. G. Christianson, Th. M. Izbicki, Brill, Leiden-New York-Köln, 1996, pp. 107–126.
HOFF, JOHANNES, *The Analogical Turn: Rethinking Modernity with Nicholas of Cusa*, Eerdmans Publishing Co., Grand Rapids, 2013.
HUDSON, NANCY J. *Becoming God. The Doctrine of Theosis in Nicholas of Cusa*, The Catholic University of America Press, Washington, D.C., 2007.
HUIZINGA, JOHAN. *Homo ludens. A Study of the Play-Element in Culture*, trans. by R. F. C. Hull, Routledge and Kegan Paul, London, 2002.
———. *The Autumn of the Middle Ages*, trans. by R. J. Payton, U. Mammitzsch, The University of Chicago Press, Chicago, 1996.
HUNDERSMARCK, LAWRENCE F. "Preaching." in: *Introducing Nicholas of Cusa. A Guide to a Renaissance Man*, eds. Ch. M. Bellito, Th. M. Izbicki, G. Christianson, Paulist Press, New York-Mahwah, NJ, 2004, pp. 232–269.
INGARDEN, ROMAN, *Man and Value*, trans. by A. Szylewicz, Philosophia Verlag, München-Wien, The Catholic University of America Press, Washington, D.C., 1983.
INGLIS, JOHN. *Spheres of Philosophical Inquiry and the Historiography of Medieval Philosophy*, Brill, Leiden-Köln-Boston, 1998.
INTRODUCING NICHOLAS OF CUSA. A Guide to a Renaissance Man, ed. Ch. M. Bellito, Th. M. Izbicki, G. Christianson, Paulist Press, New York-Mahwah, N.J., 2004.
KERGER, TOM. "La 'Cribratio Alkorani': un projet de dialogue avec l'islam." in: *Nicolas de Cues et l'islam*, ed. H. Pasqua, Peeters, Louvain-la-Neuve, Louvain-Paris, 2013, pp. 21–34.
KIJEWSKA, AGNIESZKA. "Anthropology of Gilbertus Anglicus' 'Compendium medicinae'." in: *The Embodied Soul. Aristotelian Psychology and Physiology in Medieval Europe between 1200 and 1420*, eds. M. Gensler, M. Mansfeld, M. Michałowska, Springer, Cham, Switzerland, 2022, pp. 37–56;
———. "Conception of Intellect in Eriugena and Cusanus." in: *Nicolaus Cusanus: ein bewundernswerter historischer Brennpunkt*, eds. K. Reinhardt, H. Schwaetzer, Roderer-Verlag, Regensburg, 2008, pp. 11–20.
———. "Etymology and Philosophy: God as Videns and Currens." in: *Eriugena-Cusanus*, eds. A. Kijewska, R. Majeran, H. Schwaetzer, Wydawnictwo KUL, Lublin, 2011, pp. 117–134.
———. "Human Mind as Manifestation of God's Mind in Eriugena's Philosophy." *Anuario Filosófico*, 49, n. 2, 2016, pp. 361–384.
———. "*Idiota de mente*: Cusanus' Position in the Debate between Aristotelianism and Platonism." in: *Nicholas of Cusa on the Self and Self-Consciousness*, eds. W. A. Euler, Y. Gustafsson, I. Wikström, Abo Akademi University Press, Abo, 2010, pp. 67–88.
———. "*Infinitatem te video*. La conception de l'Infinité de Dieu dans le traité *L'Icône ou la vision de Dieu*," in: *Infini et altérité dans l'oeuvre de Nicolas de Cues (1401-1464)*, ed. H. Pasqua, Peeters, Louvain-la-Neuve, 2017, pp. 185–206.

———. "Latin Neoplatonism. The Medieval Period." in: *The Oxford Handbook of Roman Philosophy*, ed. M. Garani, D. Konstan, G. Reydams-Schils, Oxford University Press, Oxford, 2023, pp. 568–582.

———. "Mathematics as a Preparation for Theology: Boethius, Eriugena, Thierry of Chartres." in: *Boèce ou la chaîne du savoirs*, ed. A. Galonnier, Peeters, Louvain-Paris, 2003, pp. 625–647.

———. "Nicolas de Cues – le philosophe de la Renaissance?." in: *Construction d'un imaginaire collectif européen. De la Renaissance aux Lumières: Allemagne, France, Pologne. Unité et diversité*, ed. L. Kańczugowski, Wydawnictwo KUL, Lublin, 2014, pp. 73–91.

———. "Scot Erigéne et Nicolas de Cues: processio et explicatio." in: Noesis. Revue philosophique du Centre de recherche d'histoire des idées, 26-27, 2016-2017: Nicolas de Cues (1401-1464). Le tournant anthroplogique de la philosophie, Université de Nice-Sophia Antipolis pp. 99–111.

———. "The history of medieval philosophy and its historiography." in: *Paradigms-Thinking Styles- Research Programs. How does science change?* ed. L. Kostuch, B. Wojciechowska, S. Konarska-Zimnicka, P. Tambor, University of Jan Kochanowski Press, Kielce, 2020, pp. 27–42.

KREMER, KURT. "Bibliographie des oeuvres de Nicolas de Cues." in: *Encyclopédie des mystiques rhénans. D'Eckhart à Nicolas de Cues et leur réception*, ed. M.-A. Vannier, Cerf, Paris, 2011, pp. 866–868.

KRETZMANN, NORMAN, KENNY, ANTHONY, PINBORG, IAN. *The Cambridge History of Later Medieval Philosophy*, Cambridge University Press, Cambridge, 1982.

KURDZIAŁEK, MARIAN. "Mediaeval Doctrines of Man as Image of the World." *Roczniki Filozoficzne*, 62, n. 4, 2014, pp. 205–246.

LESHEM, DOTAN. "Oikonomia." in: *The Routledge Handbook of Economic Theology*, ed. S. Schwarzkopf, Routledge, London-New York, 2020, pp. 272–278.

———. *The Origins of Neoliberalism. Modelling the Economy from Jesus to Foucault*, Columbia University Press, New York, 2016.

LIBERA, ALAIN DE, *La philosophie médiévale*, PUF, Paris, 1993.

———. "Le relativisme historique: théorie des *complexes questions résponses* et tratabilité." *Les Études philosophiques*, 4, 1999, pp. 479–494.

MEEKS, DOUGLAS M. "Economics in the Christian Scriptures." in: *The Oxford Handbook of Christianity and Economics*, ed. P. Oslington, Oxford University Press, Oxford, 2014, pp. 3–21.

MEUTHEN, ERICH. *Nicholas of Cusa. A Sketch for a Biography*, trans. by D. Crowner, G. Christianson, The Catholic University of America Press, Washington, D.C., 2010.

MILLER, CLYDE L. "Knowledge and Human Mind." in: *Introducing Nicholas of Cusa. A Guide to a Renaissance Man*, eds. Ch. M. Bellito, Th. M. Izbicki, G. Christianson, Paulist Press, New York-Mahwah, NJ, 2004, pp. 299–318.

———. *Reading Cusanus. Metaphor and Dialectic in a Conjectural Universe*, The Catholic University of America Press, Washington, D.C., 2003.

———. *The Art of Conjecture. Nicholas of Cusa on Knowledge*, Catholic University of America Press, Washington, D.C., 2021.

MIROY, JOVINO de GUZMAN. *Tracing Nicholas of Cusa's Early Development. The Relationship between "De concordantial catholica "and "De docta ignorantia."* Peeters, Leuven, Louvain-la-Neuve, 2009.

MONDZAIN, MARIE-JOSE. *Image, Icon, Economy. The Byzantine Origins of the Contemporary Imaginary*, trans. by R. Franses, Stanford University Press, Stanford, CA, 2005.

MONFASANI, JOHN. "Nicholas of Cusa, the Byzantines and the Greek Language." in: *Greeks and Latins in Renaissance Italy*, Variorum, Ashgate, 2004, pp. 215–252.

MORAN, DERMOT. "Nicholas of Cusa and Modern philosophy." in: *The Cambridge Companion to Renaissance Philosophy*, ed. J. Hankins, Cambridge University Press, Cambridge 2007, pp. 173–192.

MORRISSEY, THOMAS E. "The Political Philosophy of Franciscus Zabarella as Seen in His Public Addresses and Other Works." in: *Nicholas of Cusa and Times of Transition*, eds. Th. M. Izbicki, J. Aleksander, D. F. Duclow, Brill, Leiden-Boston, 2019, pp. 15–25.

MÜLLER, IRMGARD VON. "Nikolaus von Kues und die Medizin." in: *Nikolaus von Kues 1401-2001. Akten des Symposiums in Bernkastel-Kues von 23. Bis 26. Mai 2001*, eds. K. Kremer, K. Reinhardt, Paulinus Verlag, Trier, 2003, pp. 333–350.

NICHOLAS OF CUSA – A COMPANION TO HIS LIFE AND HIS TIMES, eds. M. Watanabe, G. Christianson, Th. Izbicki, Ashgate, Burlington, 2011.

NICHOLAS OF CUSA. IN SEARCH OF GOD AND WISDOM, eds. G. Christianson, Th. Izbicki, Brill, Leiden, 1991.

NICHOLAS OF CUSA AND TIMES OF TRANSITION. Essays in Honor of Gerald Christianson, eds. Th. M. Izbicki, J. Aleksander, D. F. Duclow, Brill, Leiden-Boston, 2019.

NICHOLAS OF CUSA ON CHRIST AND THE CHURCH, eds. G. Christianson, Th. M. Izbicki, Brill, Leiden-New York-Köln, 1996.

NICOLAS DE CUES ET L'ISLAM, ed. H. Pasqua, Peeters, Louvain-la-Neuve, Louvain-Paris, 2013.

NICOLLE, JEAN-MARIE. "Introduction." in: Nicolas de Cues, *Les écrits mathématiques*, ed. J.-M. Nicolle, Honoré Champion, Paris, 2007, pp. 7–69.

———. "Quelques sources philosophico-mathématiques de Nicolas de Cues," in: *Nicolas de Cues, les méthodes d'une pensées*, eds. J.-M. Counet, S. Mercier, Institute de L'Études Médiévales, Louvain-la-Neuve, 2005, pp. 47–59.

NUSSBAUM, MARTHA C. *The Therapy of Desire. Theory and Practice in Hellenistic Ethics*, Princeton University Press, Princeton, 1994.

O'BRIEN, EMILY. *The "Commentaries" of Pope Pius II (1458-1464) and the Crisis of the Fifteenth -Century Papacy*, University of Toronto Press, Toronto, Buffalo, London, 2015.

O'ROURKE, BOYLE MARJORIE. "Cusanus at Sea: The Topicality of Illuminative Discourse." *The Journal of Religion*, 71, n.2, 1991, pp. 180–210.

OSLINGTON, PAUL. "Introduction." in: *The Oxford Handbook of Christianity and Economics*, ed. P. Oslington, Oxford University Press, Oxford, 2014, pp. XIII–XVI.

PAPANIKOLAU, ARISTOTLE. "Theosis." in: *The Oxford Handbook of Mystical Theology*, ed. E. Howells, M. A. McIntosh, Oxford University Press, Oxford, 2020, pp. 569–585.

PASNAU, ROBERT, VAN DYCKE, CHRISTINA (eds.). *The Cambridge History of Medieval Philosophy*, Cambridge University Press, Cambridge, 2010.

PASQUA, HERVE. "Le Coran et le Fils de Dieu dans la 'Cribratio Alkorani'. " in: *Nicolas de Cues et l'islam*, ed. H. Pasqua, Peeters, Louvain-la-Neuve, Louvain-Paris, 2013, pp. 159–174.

PAVLAC, BRIAN A. "Nicolaus Cusanus as Prince-Bishop of Brixen (1450-1464): Historians and a Conflict of Church and State." *Historical Reflections*, 21, n. 1, 1995, pp. 131–154.

PUTALLAZ, FRANÇOIS-XAVIER. "Censorship." in: *The Cambridge History of Medieval Philosophy*, eds. R. Pasnau, Ch. Van Dyke, vol. 1, Cambridge University Press, Cambridge 2010, pp. 100–105.

RAMELLI, ILARIA L.E. "The Pastoral Epistles and Hellenistic Philosophy: 1 Timothy 5:1-2, Hierocles, and the 'Contraction of Circles'." *The Catholic Biblical Quarterly*, 73, n. 3, 2011, pp. 562–581.

REFORM, REPRESENTATION AND THEOLOGY IN NICHOLAS OF CUSA AND HIS AGE. H. L. Bond, G. Christianson (eds.), Routledge, London, New York, 2011.

REINHARDT, KLAUS. "L'idée de naissance de Dieu dans l'âme chez Nicolas de Cues et l'influence d'Eckhart." in: *La naissance de Dieu dans l'âme chez Eckhart et Nicolas de Cues*, ed. M.-A. Vannier, Cerf, Paris, 2006, pp. 85–99.

RONNOW-RASMUSSEN TONI. "Intrinsic an Extrinsic Value." in: *The Oxford Handbook of Value Theory*, eds. I. Hirose, J. Olson, Oxford University Press, Oxford, 2015, pp. 29–43.

ROSEMANN, PHILIPP W. "La philosophie et ses méthodes de recherche historique réflexions sur la dialectique entre la philosophie et son histoire." in: *Éditer, traduire, interpréter. Essais de méthodologie philosophique*, eds. S. G. Lofts, P. W. Rosemann, Peeters, Louvain-Paris, 1997, pp. 1–14.

SAINSBURY, RICHARD MARK. *Paradoxes*, 3rd edition, Cambridge University Press, Cambridge, 2009.

SCHMIDT, CARL. *Political Theology. Four Chapters on the Concept of Sovereignty*, trans. by G. Schwab, The MIT Press, Cambridge, MA, London, 1985.

SCHWARZKOPF, STEFAN. "An introduction to economic theology." in: *The Routledge Handbook of Economic Theology*, ed. S. Schwarzkopf, Routledge, London-New York, 2020, pp. 1–15.

SENGER, HANS G. "Jeu de la boule." in: *Encyclopédie des mystiques rhénans. D'Eckhart à Nicolas de Cues et leur réception*, ed. M.-A. Vannier, Cerf, Paris, 2011, pp. 675–677.

———. "Praefatio editoris." in: Nicolai de Cusa, *De ludo globi, Opera omnia* vol. IX, ed. H. G. Senger, Felix Meiner Verlag, Hamburgi 1998, pp. IX–XLII.

SEŃKO, WŁADYSŁAW, WŁODEK, ZOFIA. "Les manuscrits des oeuvres de Nicolas de Cues conservés en Pologne." *Mediaevalia Philosophica Polonorum*, 13, 1968, pp. 82–99.

SIGMUND, PAUL E. "Introduction." in: *Nicholas of Cusa, The Catholic Concordance*, trans. by P. E. Sigmund, Cambridge University Press, Cambridge, 1991, pp. XI–XLVI.

———. *Nicholas of Cusa and Medieval Political Thought*, Harvard University Pres, Cambridge MA, 1963.

SINGH, DEVIN. *Divine Currency. The Theological Power of Money in the West*, Stanford University Press, Stanford, CA, 2018.

STEENBERGHEN, FERNAND VAN, *La philosophie au XIIIe siècle*, Publications Universitaires, Louvain, Béatrice-Nauwelaerts, Paris, 1966.

STIEBER, JOACHIM. "The Hercules of the Eugenians' at the Crossroads: Nicholas of Cusa's Decision for the Pope Against the Council in 1436-37 – Theological, Political, and Social Aspect." in: *Nicholas of Cusa. In Search of God and Wisdom*, eds. G. Christianson, Th. Izbicki, Brill, Leiden, 1991, pp. 221–255.

STRAUSS, GERALD. "Ideas of 'Reformatio' and 'Renovatio' from the Middle Ages to the Reformation." in: *Handbook of European History, 1400-1600: Late Middle Ages, Renaissance, and Reformation*, vol. II: *Visions, Programs and Outcomes*, eds. Th. A. Brady. H. A. Oberman, J. D. Tracy, Brill, Leiden, 1995, pp. 2–30.

STRUCK, PETER T. *Birth of the Symbol: Ancient Readers at the Limits of Their Texts*, Princeton University Press, Princeton, 2004.

STUMP, ELEONORE. *Atonement*, Oxford University Press, Oxford, 2018.

———. *Wandering in Darkness. Narrative and the Problem of Suffering*, Oxford University Press, Oxford, 2010.

SULLIVAN, DONALD. "Cusanus and Pastoral Renewal: The Reform of Popular Religion in the Germanies." in: *Nicholas of Cusa on Christ and the Church*, eds. G. Christianson, Th. M. Izbicki, Brill, Leiden-New York-Köln, 1996, pp. 165–173.

ŚMIST, ANTONI. *"Łów mądrości" jako ćwiczenie duchowe. Transcendentalno-anagogiczna interpretacja filozofii Mikołaja z Kuzy*. Academicon, Lublin, 2023.

TANAKA, JULIE K. "From universal to local: German Identity in Nicholas of Cusa's Catholic Concordance." *Renaissance Studies*, 36, n. 2, 2021, pp. 295–312.

TANNER, KATHRYN. *Economy of Grace*, Fortress Press, Minneapolis, 2005.

THE ROUTLEDGE HANDBOOK OF ECONOMIC THEOLOGY, ed. S. Schwarzkopf, Routledge, London-New York, 2020.

VANSTEENBERGHE, EDMOND. *Le cardinal Nicolas de Cues*, Honoré Champion, Paris 1920 (repr. Minerva GMBH, Frankfurt am Main, 1963).

WATANABE, MORIMICHI. "Political and Legal Ideas." in: *Introducing Nicholas of Cusa. A Guide to a Renaissance Man*, eds. Ch. M. Bellito, Th. M. Izbicki, G. Christianson, Paulist Press, New York-Mahwah, NJ, 2004, pp. 141–165.

WATTS, PAULINE M. "Renaissance Humanism." in: *Introducing Nicholas of Cusa. A Guide to a Renaissance Man*, eds. Ch. M. Bellito, Th. M. Izbicki, G. Christianson, Paulist Press, New York-Mahwah, NJ, 2004, pp. 169–204.

WILLIAMS, ROWAN. "Theology as a way of life." in: *The Practice of the Presence of God. Theology as a way of life*, eds. M. Laird, S. T. Hidden, Routledge, London, New York, 2017, pp. 11–16.

ZOHAR, DANAH, MARSHALL, IAN. *Spiritual Intelligence. The Ultimate Intelligence*, Bloomsbury, London-New York-Berlin-Sydney, 2012 (e-book).

ZUPKO, JACK, Buridan, John, 1998, DOI:10.4324/9780415249126-B022-1. Routledge Encyclopedia of Philosophy, Taylor and Francis, Routledge, https://www.rep.routledge.com/articles/biographical/buridan-john-c-1300-after-1358/v-1.

Index